MEDICINE THAT MOVES YOU

MEDICINE THAT MOVES YOU

HOW PHYSICAL ACTIVITY CAN HELP HEAL YOU IN MORE WAYS THAN YOU THINK

SIMON WAHBA

NEW DEGREE PRESS

MEDICINE THAT MOVES YOU

How physical activity can help heal you in more ways than you think

ISBN

978-1-64137-360-9   *Paperback*

978-1-64137-700-3   *Ebook*

*To my mom, dad, and brother who always inspire
me to be the best version of myself.*

CONTENTS

"The doctor of the future will give no medicine, but will involve the patient in the proper use of food, fresh air, and exercise."

—THOMAS EDISON

GETTING THE MOST OUT OF YOUR EXPERIENCE

Treat this book as a cheat sheet on the effects of physical activity and how it can change different aspects of your life for the better. It is broken down into three parts: physical, mental, and social health benefits. Each part takes a subcategory from these three major topics and dives deeper into the subject examining the specific effects physical activity has for that particular body system or health sphere. Here is the list of topics that will make navigating the book easier:

ZERO IN ON WHAT MATTERS TO YOU:

Life can be complicated and we are all faced with our own unique set of issues and health concerns. Although this book gives insight on how being active can benefit your body as a whole, please feel free to skip to chapters that pertain more directly to what matters to you.

GO FOR THE HOLISTIC APPROACH:

Once you have started to learn about how you can take back autonomy over your health in the specific sections you choose, push forward and learn about how exercise can affect other parts of your body that you may not have been as concerned with. Understanding all the benefits of physical activity will not only help you be better equipped when something goes wrong, but it will also help you be more consistent in achieving weekly goals by making exercise a priority in your life.

MAKE THE CHANGE:

Once you learn about the importance of being active, then it's time to start implementing it into your life. Give it a try and put what you've learned to the test so you can actually feel the difference exercise can have on your quality of life.

INTRODUCTION

Every year the US government discloses its annual mortality report, and for the first time since the influenza pandemic of 1918, life expectancy has gone down in two out of the last three years[1][2].Yes, this means that people from the US are now living shorter lives than their parents. This is incredibly frightening and, on the surface level, doesn't make any sense being that our medicinal techniques and knowledge are only getting better with time.

In fact, the US has the largest healthcare budget of any nation by far. The Centers for Medicare and Medicaid Services (CMS) estimates the US spending to be $3.5 trillion just last

---

1   "NVSS - Mortality Data". 2019. Cdc.Gov.
2   Santhanam, Laura, and Laura Santhanam. 2018. "American Life Expectancy Has Dropped Again. Here's Why". PBS Newshour.

year alone[3]. This amounts to about $10,224 per person, which is almost twice the global average and almost $2,000 more than Switzerland, which is second in healthcare spending per capita[4]. Yet despite the amount of money we spend, why are we now seeing our lifespan decrease?

Many people point to the obesity rate trends that we have seen in the past few decades. Nearly 40 percent of Americans are now obese, and it's not just adults, the number of obese children has also been continuously on the rise. Today, 30 percent of our youth are either overweight or obese. Obesity itself is responsible for costing $147 billion in medical costs and only continues to rise.[5] Others point to the increase in drug usage and, consequently, drug overdoses because there was a 10 percent increase in the number of people who died from drug overdoses from 2016 to 2017. The amount of suicides in the US have also gone up, increasing 3.7 percent from last year[6].

The cause of these diseases is multivariable and pinpointing a specific cause would be tricky, but there is a common

3   "Historical - Centers For Medicare & Medicaid Services". 2019. Cms.Gov. Accessed October 10 2019.

4   "How Does Health Spending In The U.S. Compare To Other Countries? - Peterson-Kaiser Health System Tracker". 2019. Peterson-Kaiser Health System Tracker.

5   "Economic Costs Of Obesity | Healthy Communities For A Healthy Future". 2019.

6   "Faststats-Leading Causes of Death". 2019. Cdc.Gov.

denominator between them. The chance of getting any of these conditions is much higher if you are inactive.

Things begin to make sense as only 23 percent of Americans meet weekly guidelines for aerobic and muscle-strengthening activities[7]. This puts the majority of Americans at risk for these diseases and many more, but if being inactive is the cause, wouldn't being active be the solution? Unfortunately, the reality is that although the answer seems so straightforward—just exercise—it is much more complicated than that.

Exercise.

The word itself is synonymous with so many emotions that aren't always on the same side of the spectrum.

On one hand, you have people who hate it. The very word irks them to the core because it reminds them of what they are not. They feel they haven't reached the "expectations" set by society to have that hourglass figure, or to be able to bench a house above their chest. They feel suffocated by the requirements to be beautiful, even though many are unrealistic to achieve and, in turn, view themselves as lesser because of it.

---

7   "Faststats-Exercise or Physical Activity". 2019. Cdc.Gov.

At that point who can blame someone for hating exercise when every time they try to start, they are discouraged with thoughts of "I can't," or "it's impossible," when wondering if they'll ever look like the computer altered pictures they see in the magazines.

Others are indifferent about it.

Some feel like they just don't have the time and with juggling work, family, and whatever other commitments may be in the way; they just don't think it's that important. They feel like sacrificing the time to go to the gym or for a run is well worth the extra hours at the office, or watching the game live on TV instead of on a recording. Some people would just rather get the extra thirty minutes of sleep, and it's not hard to blame them when they have to wake up for school or work at 6:00 a.m. every day.

While all these are fair reasons, there are still those people who do it even with all the complications of their lives. They'll get up early and plan it into their schedules because exercise makes them feel free. Free from distractions that plague them during their working hours, whether that be the stress of a job, making ends meet, a test at school, or whatever else may be in the way. Physical activity has the power to erase all that negativity and stress that the day can bring upon you as your body becomes more preoccupied with healing rather than hurting.

Others love the freedom it gives them to enjoy their favorite activities. Whether that be going on a hike with friends, golfing, or just out for a quick run. Being active also gives people the freedom to take care of miscellaneous tasks around the house such as cleaning, gardening, or even just being able to get out of bed and go to the bathroom in the morning.

Although it seems like an easy task, people are now struggling to complete these essential activities for daily living such as getting out of bed and brushing their teeth. Americans are now more disabled than ever before as the percentage of people who have a disability has steadily grown since 2010[8]. Many people would think that this is mostly due to the percentage of older adults increasing, but what's shocking is that the majority of disabled Americans are in the working class from ages eighteen to sixty-four[9]. A large portion of these disabilities are exasperated by sedentary activity and many could have been mitigated or even prevented if the person had been more physically active throughout their lives[10].

---

8   "2017 Disability Statistics Annual Report" Disabilitycompendium. Org. Accessed October 11 2019.

9   Ibid

10   "Physical Activity Guidelines for Americans". Health.Gov.

Physical activity is the key to longevity for our bodies. It isn't until we are educated about it or experience its medicinal effects firsthand that we understand how important physical activity really is.

* * *

In fact, the implications of being active has been known for centuries. As far back as 300 BC, Hippocrates, nicknamed the "father of western medicine," said, "If we could give every individual the right amount of nourishment and exercise, not too little and not too much, we would have found the safest way to health.[11]" Let's not forget that he came to this conclusion without having the fancy tools we have today. No machines that can track heart rate, no gadgets to measure body fat percentage, but just his own two eyes and the observation of people around him. Over 2,000 years later, he could not have been more correct.

Most of all, this shows a major issue in how we have adapted as a whole. Today, we still don't view exercise as "the safest way to health," and although people know it makes you feel "healthier," it still isn't viewed as a medicine, instead it's viewed as something more supplemental to do on the side.

---

11 Tipton, Charles M. 2014. "The History Of "Exercise Is Medicine" In Ancient Civilizations". Advances In Physiology Education 38 (2): 109-117. American Physiological Society.

This is a critical mistake in how we think and it needs to be fixed or we will continue to see health trends all over the world getting worse.

The fact is that physical activity is a medicine for our bodies that we should be taking daily. It is a medicine that is natural, holistic, and affects you from head to toe as soon as you start to do it. What's even more impressive is that no medicine can encompass so many benefits in one "pill" like being active can. These scope from the bigger things like decreasing your chance of getting certain cancers or dementia, to the little things like regulating blood pressure, heart rate, or even boosting dopamine levels in the brain just to make you feel happier. The best part is that the benefits to your sleep, mood, and function start immediately, so any little bit helps[12].

Even with all these reasons to start being more active, people still can't seem to stick to their new year's resolutions and go to the gym or eat healthier. A survey taken by people from every state found that 49.9 percent of people have some type of health-related resolution, but only 63 percent of Americans stick to that through the end of the first month[13]. This could be due to the fact that our perspective on why we

---

12 Physical Activity Guidelines for Americans". Health.Gov.
13 "The Most Popular 2019 New Year's Resolutions | Vitagene". 2018.

exercise in the first place is skewed. Instead of doing it for your own health benefit, people do it because they may be self-conscious of how they appear and are scared they might be called "fat" or "ugly."

Although these thoughts motivate you to go for the first week, it's hard to be consistent when your motivation is fear, rather than the pursuit of health. Moving our mind-set from being extrinsically motivated by other people's opinions to being intrinsically motivated by your own desire to live longer, is the key to breaking out of the cycle of falling into old habits that have plagued us for so long.

Still, it won't be easy because there will be many obstacles along the way to change the minds of so many. Big corporations who have money-making agendas, groups who will dismiss the data as lies, and even your own self-doubt are just a few things that will hinder this initiative. That is why it is our responsibility, as those who know the facts, to continue to push for education in schools and continue to do as much research as possible to come up with undeniable evidence for exercise as a mental, physical, and social remedy.

* * *

Exercise is medicine.

My own personal life has made it clear to me—as you'll read more in the book—both of my parents lives were nearly taken when doctors and the health system didn't include physical activity as a part of their daily prescription.

This book aims to change that.

I want each of us to begin to see how exercise is no different than taking our daily pills for what ails us. If we miss a pill, it could greatly affect our lives. Similarly, if we don't include physical activity, it could greatly affect our lives.

Research teams from Harvard, Stanford, and the University of London ran an analysis of sixteen major studies and 305 randomized trials to see if exercise could really be as effective as a pill. After screening results from over 300,000 people they found evidence to "suggest that exercise and many drug interventions are often potentially similar in terms of reducing mortality during rehabilitation after stroke, prevention of diabetes and secondary prevention of coronary heart disease.[14]"

In fact, heart failure was the only condition that was observed to fair better with pills than exercise. Now, to say that

---

14 Naci, H., and J. P. A. Ioannidis. 2013. "Comparative Effectiveness Of Exercise And Drug Interventions On Mortality Outcomes: Metaepidemiological Study".

everyone should stop taking their medications would be a gross misinterpretation of the results, but instead this study shows that exercise can be effective as a medicine and that we should commit more resources to learning how it can help benefit our lives.

This idea that exercise is medicine was popularized in the 1980s by Dr. Robert Butler as he famously said, "if exercise could be packed into a pill, it would be the single most widely prescribed and beneficial medicine in the nation.[15]" Now, almost forty years later, he could not have been more correct, as new data continues to support the increased use of exercise as a remedy for depression, neurodegenerative diseases like Alzheimer's, cardiovascular diseases, and more regarding many body systems[16].

When reports first came out about how bad cigarettes were for your health, no one wanted to believe it. It was only until concrete evidence was exhaustingly placed in front of policy makers that a change was implemented. In many ways similar to cigarettes, exercise, or rather the lack of it, is the next big healthcare topic that needs attention.

Most importantly, we have to teach our youth about the necessity of exercise because they are the ones who will

15 Publishing, Harvard. 2019. "What We Do—And Don't—Know About Exercise - Harvard Health". Harvard Health.
16 "Physical Activity Guidelines for Americans". Health.Gov.

collectively make the change to what society deems as important. Now, we still have a long way to go, but there have been efforts in the past to try to encourage more kids to become active. In 1966, President Lyndon B. Johnson created the Presidential Fitness Challenge, which was a set of fitness tests such as sit-ups, push-ups, and a mile run, designed to test the fitness levels of the American youth. If a student was to place in the top fifteenth percentile for each activity, then they would be rewarded with the Presidential Fitness Award to acknowledge their achievement[17].

President Johnson hoped that by placing an award up for grabs, students would work harder and compete with one another and although it helped some students become more active, others found the tests boring and embarrassing, especially students who weren't as athletically developed yet. Although it had its problems, at least it was a start, as emphasis finally began to be placed on youth development.

The most important time to build healthy habits comes when we are kids. The opposite also applies here, as a study of over 7,000 kids, published in the New England Journal of Medicine, found that one-third of children who were overweight in kindergarten became obese by third grade[18]. What's worse

17 "Award Program Information". 2012. HHS.Gov.
18 "Incidence Of Childhood Obesity In The United States | NEJM". 2019. New England Journal Of Medicine.

is that every year after that, their chance of correcting their weight issue became smaller and smaller.

For this reason, teaching the exercise benefits to kids, as well as finding ways to fit more physical activity into their daily routine, is essential. Whether that be by planning short bursts of activity during class time or even incentivizing team or individual sport participation, there can be ways to help kids be healthy from an early age. The Institute for the Study of Youth Sports found that kids who were active in at least one sport will have a smaller chance of developing diabetes, obesity, and depression. Children who played a sport were also less susceptible to drug and alcohol abuse, have better grades in school, and acquire key social skills for the future[19].

These social skills help children communicate and help contribute to a feeling of belonging amongst their group members during sport participation. These feelings also invoke a sense of self-confidence, which raises self-esteem as well. The social benefits aren't just for developing members of the youth, as people from all over the world can learn a thing or two through the power of sports.

Exercise can also be a social medicine of sorts for a country that is so desperate for unity. Sports and exercise can be ways

---

19   Sports Participation And Drug Use Among Young People In Mauritius". 2019. International Journal Of Adolescence And Youth.

to bring us together as a community. Aside from the cognitive and physical benefits for youth development, exercise creates team bonds which can often resemble one similar to an actual family, and sometimes even be there for people who don't have what some consider a "normal family." The feeling of empathy and compassion for one another is something that is bred through team-oriented activities and something that can help heal a nation that is divided, all while making each of us healthier and allowing us to live longer in harmony.

This book is for those who didn't get that opportunity to learn before and to strengthen those ideas for people who have already been exposed to some of the life-changing effects of exercise. You'll learn the best exercise prescription, fit exactly for you, so that you stick to these new habits and change your lifestyle.

As you dive deeper into this book, you'll hear from physicians and scientists from various departments in top research institutions such as NYU, Harvard, UNC, Yale, and you'll learn more about the effects exercise has on major body parts such as your heart and lungs. You'll learn insight about how professional athletes, such as Kevin Love and Demar Derozan, use sports to cope with mental illnesses, and even learn how some scientists believe that exercise actually has the ability to change how your mind sees the world.

We'll also look at people with hereditary conditions like Romeo Dev, the world's smallest body builder, who uses physical activity to combat the health complication of his rare condition. You'll even get information from policy makers in education and political systems to see how we are trying to make being active more accessible to all groups and how they implement physical activity during the school and work day.

So, with benefits to your immediate and long-term health, as well as the power to unite a nation diseased with hatred for one another, there doesn't seem to be a limit as to what exercise can do for us as a society. Yes, being active is that powerful for us as a nation and on an individual level. Even famous Vietnamese monk and peace activist, Thich Nhat Hanh, says, "When it comes to health and well-being, regular exercise is about as close to a magic potion as you can get.[20]"

Maybe the issue has been that in our pursuit to create a cure for the millions of diseases in existence, we forget to look at the tools we already have, and one of those underappreciated tools is being physically active.

I hope this book helps be the catalyst for change in some-body's lifestyle, even if it's just one person, because one

20 "Benefits Of Regular Exercise - Imagine Health". 2019. Imagine Health.

person is enough to start the revolution to give millions of people across the world a sense of freedom and the ability to take ownership of their lives. Exercise has been the answer that has always been right in front of us. Now is the time to realize that and change for the better.

WHEN EXERCISE
BECAME MEDICINE

———

Growing up in Egypt in the seventies, my dad did two things more than anything: study and run around. Truthfully, if he had it his way, he would spend all day playing outside, but his dad never let him do anything until he finished his homework. Even when temperatures reached above one hundred degrees, he would still rush home from school just to finish his work, so he could sprint to meet his friends on the neighborhood field.

My dad's first love was definitely soccer. He described the pitch as his "paradise." He loved the endless opportunity that came with all the space of the field, the ball, and the net.

His adoration for the game kept him playing through college and even after he moved to New York and started a family.

I remember him taking me to the field where he played with friends from the neighborhood and he would come to me after the game and show me how to juggle and shoot. You couldn't wipe the grin off my face as he kicked the ball as high up in the air as he could, and I remember thinking that it might never come down. I wanted to kick like that, I wanted to be like him.

My dad also introduced me to my first love, which was the game of basketball. For Christmas, he got me a Fisher-Price basketball hoop and I became obsessed after my first shot. I wouldn't leave him alone, even after a long day of work, begging him to play one-on-one with me, and even though he won most of the time, he let me get a few points every once in a while.

Him sacrificing his relaxation hours to run around with my brother and I at night is what got us started in sports and we never looked back. Our parents strongly encouraged us to be active, even if it wasn't soccer, which was a big reason why we got involved in so many different activities as kids.

This is not uncommon as researchers have observed this association between parent-child behaviors for a long time. For example, parental eating habits have a great amount of influence on the eating habits of their children[2122]. This makes sense, as food availability and eating habits are derived from the parents because they make all the purchases and decisions. This can be a problem in the future if a family doesn't lead a healthy lifestyle, as habits stick with these children as they grow up. Another study, done by the University of Idaho, also found these trends as they surveyed over 500 college kids to see how their eating habits compared to their youth. Not surprisingly, these individuals seemed to eat similarly to how they used to at home, and those who ate healthier at home generally also ate healthier in college and vice versa[23].

Studies also support the same correlation between parents and their kids when it comes to things such as study habits, brushing their teeth, and reading, to name a few[24]. These trends suggest that children are more likely to follow a lifestyle choice if their parents do them as well.

Naturally, the same principle applies to physical activity levels.

---

21 "Home Food Availability, Parental Dietary Intake, And Familial Eating Habits Influence The Diet Quality Of Urban Hispanic Children | Childhood Obesity".

22 Branen, Laurel, and Janice Fletcher. 1999. "Comparison Of College Students' Current Eating Habits And Recollections Of Their Childhood Food Practices". Journal Of Nutrition Education 31

23 Ibid

24 "Parental Influence On Children's Oral Health-Related Behavior". 2019. Acta Odontologica Scandinavica.

A Duke University study followed families in North Carolina for a week to see if that was really the case. They equipped parents and their children each with accelerometers that they were required to wear twenty-four hours a day for one week to track their activity levels. They found that parents with higher totals of weekly physical activity were more likely to have children with higher totals as well[25]. The research team at Oregon State University also found that the amount of movement that parents would partake in also influenced the amount of physical activity their preschool children got[26].

Still, there are times when children can be stubborn, I know this because I was one of those kids at one point too. The reality is some kids are just not going to be interested in playing a team sport, which is completely fine as long as they stay active in other ways.

Other children won't have the opportunity to be involved in team sports due to financial and accessibility issues. Whether it be because of the cost of equipment, league fees, or even not having a community league in the first place, they are deprived of those learning experiences that come with youth sports.

---

25 Fuemmeler, Bernard F, Cheryl B Anderson, and Louise C Mâsse. 2011. "Parent-Child Relationship Of Directly Measured Physical Activity". International Journal Of Behavioral Nutrition And Physical Activity

26 Loprinzi, Paul D., and Stewart G. Trost. 2010. "Parental Influences On Physical Activity Behavior In Preschool Children". Preventive Medicine

These experiences not only help facilitate cognitive and social development in children, but also help build important habits. Kids who didn't get these chances don't build these habits and, therefore, don't see the importance of being active. For them it will take another type of catalyst to change their perception. Some find this through experience, whether good or bad, while others are fortunate enough to learn about the multitude of benefits that exercise has to offer in school or through personal research.

As a kid, I was very shy and I loved being on different sports teams because it forced me to be social in a way I felt comfortable. This feeling of belonging kept me playing sports for a long time, but I played more for the social experience rather than thinking about doing it for my health.

That didn't really change for me until my junior year of high school. All within a year and a half, my dad suffered a brain hemorrhage and discovered that he needed a heart valve replacement, while my mother lost the function in her last healthy kidney and was also diagnosed with breast cancer. We had a family history of things such as hypertension and high cholesterol, so I wasn't too surprised. Instead I was scared. What would happen to my family and what could I have done to help them?

Thankfully, with the help of many doctors and the support of loved ones, my dad made a full recovery and my mom is now living happily on dialysis and is cancer free. Although out of harm's way for the moment, the feeling of fear never left me for the rest of high school and later on into my life. Remembering how much pain they were in was the wake-up call that I needed to make a change in my life.

* * *

I committed myself to exercising more, but what does exercise really even mean? The American Council on Exercise (ACE) defines it as planned, structured, and repetitive movements intended to improve physical fitness[27]. This isn't to say that unplanned and unstructured activities have no benefits. In fact, any physical activity, even just standing, can help circulation, focus, and boost your metabolism. Not everyone will be able to go to the gym and do what we think of as exercise, but those who can't do not have to fear. As long as they are physically active to what they are capable of, they can receive a multitude of benefits.

With so many positive effects that being active has to offer, why don't we consider it a medicine? By examining the definition of medicine more closely, we begin to see why people don't associate exercise with it. Merriam-Webster defines medicine as a substance or preparation used in treating

27 Dominique Gummelt, PhD. 2015. "Physical Activity Vs. Exercise: What'S The Difference?". Acefitness.Org.

disease[28]. First, we see the word substance is used in the beginning of the sentence. This is a problem because it doesn't encompass action, rather it refers more to pills and artificially made objects. The definition also points to the time in which we use medicine, which would be after to treat the disease. This is another issue because it dismisses the entire preventive aspect of medicine that exercise is especially good at.

For this reason we need to redefine the term medicine to include any action that helps benefit health and well-being. This way we can encompass all the preventative and reactive tactics to diseases we use, and more importantly get people to understand that exercise belongs in that category.

* * *

That change came for me soon after the health crisis with my father. I remember going to the cardiologists with my him following his procedure. The doctor came in and asked my dad all sorts of questions and then began outlining my dad's rehabilitation plan to get him back to full strength.

He explained that the heart was a muscle and that to preserve his new valve, he needed to make sure his heart was fit, that way there was little stress placed on it. He even said that his

---

28   "Definition Of DOCTOR". 2019. Merriam-Webster.Com.

lack of activity could have played a major role in this happening in the first place.

At that very moment is where I reached my epiphany for how I view exercise. To think that what happened to my dad could have been prevented got me obsessed with finding out just how physical activity could be used to help prevent such terrible things from happening to him.

From that day on, I began to think about what the doctor said anytime I went to the gym or practice. I would always push myself a little harder because I knew that I didn't ever want to face such daunting health concerns. It wasn't just the fear of these conditions either, as I wanted to make sure I would always have the freedom to move around freely later on in my life.

* * *

It's hard to build new habits, but it's even harder to break old ones. Just like with new year's resolutions, most people don't get past the first three weeks of their new lifestyle changes. Although there is no perfect way to start a new exercise plan, it is possible.

Take Michael Allon for example. Allon weighed 264 pounds at one point and struggled to move around his house. His weight contributed to his self-esteem issues until one day he decided he had enough. Never having any serious swimming experience, Allon committed himself to swimming three to four times a week and the results began to speak for themselves. He noticed his, "energy increase" and in one year he lost 100 pounds. When asked how he made this change he said his key was consistency and finding something he loved to do. He also stressed that, "it's good to have a plan. That plan doesn't have to be hard, just start with a small change.[29]"

Being active doesn't mean committing yourself to going to a gym, you can find other activities you enjoy such as swimming, climbing, fishing, and so much more that you can do instead and still receive all the benefits that come with being physically active. Making exercise a hobby can be key to unlocking consistency in your exercise regimen.

* * *

I also saw what inactivity could do to a person. Following surgery, my mom struggled getting around because her condition left her sidelined for a while. Going up and down steps or even just standing for too long became increasingly uncomfortable for her. She would be heartbroken that she couldn't go support my brother and I at sporting events

---

29 "How I Lost 100 Lbs Swimming 4X/Week | (Michael Allon) #Askaswimpro Show"

because most of the time there was no room in the bleachers to sit. I insisted that I knew what she was going through, and that it wasn't her fault, but you could still tell that she was disappointed. Seeing her deterioration hurt her motivation to get back to where she was pre-surgery and I hated to see her struggle. The fact was that due to her lack of exercise, her quality of life had been diminished, and her risk of diseases had increased. For someone who has sacrificed so much for me, I knew that I needed to help her understand how badly she needed to get moving as much as possible.

I started to ask her to go on walks around the block with me or put her favorite music on so she could dance around the house. I even got our family a dog so my parents would be forced to walk her and be active throughout the day. Any activity that I could use to sneak exercise into their daily routines, I would do, no matter how much or how little.

As we walked the dog together and I would often bore her with as many exercise facts as I could remember from the internet, hoping that just one of them would be the one to get her obsessed about being healthy. I think she felt like I nagged her at times, but even though she was annoyed, she knew what I was trying to do, and I could always sense the appreciation that she felt because I cared about her. Thankfully, my nagging eventually paid off and she agreed to come to the gym with me.

I remember her look of apprehension as she walked in through the doors for the first time. She had never really gone to the gym before and didn't even know where to start. The gym can be a scary place filled with judgement and comparison, so I understood her feelings. Still, we pushed on together and the more exercises we did, the more she felt comfortable being there. Slowly, her workouts became longer, she became stronger and her attitude of "I can't" became an "I can" instead. Suddenly, she could walk around town after dinner without getting tired, she felt less pain in her knees, and she was able to go up and down the stairs without putting two feet on each step for the first time in years following her surgery.

Her body was finally starting to adapt and she felt so much better because of it. Her progress was slow and it took years of convincing to finally get her to come with me. After only a few times at the gym, I finally caught her smiling afterward. I asked her what she was so happy about jokingly, and her answered shocked me. She said she felt good inside, like she had another type of energy she had never tapped into before. She was sore all over, but felt great. I remember telling her this was the "power of exercise," but looking back I think it was something more than that for her. That was the moment where her perspective on being active finally switched. She finally began to understand she needed it if she wanted to have autonomy over the rest of her life, to do what she wanted without restrictions, to be free.

I tell you these personal accounts because, unlike me, I want everyone who reads this to change their perspective on how useful physical activity can be instead of waiting for some type of traumatic experience, injury, or disease to show them the importance being active is for your health.

Truthfully, I am one of the lucky ones who still has their parents, despite their struggles with certain conditions and, thankfully, they have finally started to take their health more seriously. However, everyone is not as lucky and many have lost loved ones due to the lack of education and attention physically activity gets in education systems, the media, and in everyday life.

Only recently has attention been brought to this issue, as new studies show undeniable evidence on the positive health effects moving around has on our bodies, no matter what stage of life you're in. The more time that passes, the more evidence we find supporting this claim, but it doesn't take a modern-day scientist to know how impactful exercise can really be for you.

PART 1

PHYSICAL HEALTH

CHAPTER 1

THE EXERCISE PRESCRIPTION

—

On December 3, 2005, fifteen-year-old boy, DJ Little, was crossing the street right in front of his home and was hit by a car. The impact threw him several feet and damaged several of his bones and organs, putting him in a coma. Doctors gave him little chance to survive the first twenty-four hours and even if he woke up, they told his parents that he would be a "vegetable" at best. His parents will tell you that DJ was "stubborn" and he refused to give up[30].

After undergoing seventeen different surgeries, he finally woke up and began his mission to rehab with one goal; to walk at his graduation.

---

30 Thomas, Sue. 2011. "The Power Of Physical Therapy: One Student's Story Of Brain Injury And Recovery"

To give him back his mobility, DJ would embark on a very long road where physical therapy would be essential to his recovery. It is kind of counterintuitive that moving a damaged part of your body around actually helps you recover, but slow and monitored activity is imperative in allowing the mind and muscles to reestablish important neural connections. Physical therapy is one of the most obvious uses for exercise as medicine because through movement your body begins to heal.

The use of physical therapy began in the early 1800s, when Per Henrik Ling used to use therapeutic tactics to help the Swedish gymnastic team perform at the highest level. Following in their footsteps, more teams, and eventually more people around the world began using these therapeutic techniques to help rehabilitate injury and gain maximum performance out of each patient or client[31]. It wasn't until 1921 that the first official organization dealing with this kind of practice was created, they were called the American Women's Physical Therapeutic Association. Men were eventually permitted in the association, and during World War II their members were in large demand because they were needed to help aid and rehabilitate soldiers coming back with war injuries. The polio epidemic was also

31 Shaik, AbdulRahim, and ArakkalManiyat Shemjaz. 2014. "The Rise Of Physical Therapy: A History In Footsteps". Archives Of Medicine And Health Sciences

gearing up at that time, keeping the fewer than 1,000 members very busy as they aimed to combat the effects of muscle atrophy caused by polio[32].

We have come a long way since then, there are now more than 95,000 members in the American Physical Therapy Association (APTA). Physical therapists now treat a variety of ailments including cardiopulmonary diseases like chronic obstructive pulmonary disease (COPD) or musculoskeletal injuries from sports, work, or just everyday life. Physical therapists can also treat neurological issues found after a stroke and can help build the mind muscle connection that will allow a recovering patient to walk again[33].

In fact, physical therapy (PT) can often be just as good as surgical options. A study done by Anthony Delitto, chairman of the department of physical therapy at the University of Pittsburgh, wanted to test the effect of surgery versus physical therapy on older patients with spinal stenosis. The two-year study studied 169 patients who were fifty years or older and randomly assigned them to either a group who would have a surgical procedure done or to PT twice a week for six weeks. Delitto found that, "there were no detectable

32 Ibid
33 American Physical Therapy Association. 2019. "About Physical Therapist (PT) Careers". Apta.Org

differences between the groups in how their pain abated and the degree to which function was restored."[34]

The power of PT and movement in general has the ability to help us heal in ways we didn't think possible, even providing us the same effect of a procedure in this case, without all the complications of surgery. It is by no means a magic solution, but with consistency, many recovering patients accomplished things that their doctor's may not have thought attainable after the injury.

This was exactly the case for DJ, as at the start of his rehabilitation, he couldn't even roll over in bed without help. Yet he was determined to see the process through and continued to go to therapy, missing as little sessions as possible. Four years later, DJ was finally able to take a lap around the kitchen and will be able to walk during his graduation[35].

His family credits his commitment to his physical and occupational therapy sessions as being what helped him make such big strides and this is hardly the first or the last story that shows how physical activity can help heal someone after a major injury. If the body isn't moving around, it will just

34 Finder, Chuck, and Anthony Delitto. 2019. "Physical Therapy, Surgery Produce Same Results For Spinal Stenosis In Older Patients | Pitt Chronicle | University Of Pittsburgh". Chronicle.Pitt.Edu

35 Thomas, Sue. 2011. "The Power Of Physical Therapy: One Student's Story Of Brain Injury And Recovery". Mlive.Com.

be rotting away, but if one keeps active, the body can be preoccupied with healing rather than hurting.

PHYSICAL ACTIVITY AND QUALITY OF LIFE

Physical activity in general has the power to drastically increase your quality of life and protect your longevity. It will help you keep participating in your favorite activities, as well as allow you to accomplish essential tasks for your everyday life. The term medicine is often thought of as something that is given to someone who is sick, but another scope to medicine is the preventive aspect of it, which focuses on keeping people from getting sick or injured in the first place.

That is where getting exercise really shines as being physical activity that can help decrease your risk of getting multiple diseases. According to the physical activity guidelines (PAG), a report issued by the US department of health, the risk for you to acquire various amounts of diseases are reduced just by being active.

They report that "diseases such as coronary heart disease, stroke, cancer at multiple sites, type 2 diabetes, obesity, hypertension, and osteoporosis," are all under the long list of diseases that can be prevented by moving around[36].

---

36 "Physical Activity Guidelines for Americans 2nd Edition". Health.Gov.

The PAG also highlights the regulatory effects that moving around has to offer. Individuals who are active have more consistent sleep patterns, improve focus, reduced anxiety and stress, and even help improve and maintain cognition, which is especially important as you get older[37].

As you age your chance for certain neurodegenerative diseases like Parkinson's Disease (PD) increases. Dr. Hirsch, the senior scientist at Carolina Healthcare Systems, conducted an analysis of multiple studies dealing with cohorts with PD and various types of exercise interventions. PD doesn't have a cure, but Dr. Hirsch believed that exercise could potentially slow the progression of the conditions. He found that one hundred patients across six studies had higher observable levels of BDNF (a protein that is gradually lost during the progression of PD), helping to show some benefits of the relationship between being active and brain health longevity[38].

It's amazing to see the many ways that being active can give you your freedom back, even when modern pharmaceutical methods and surgical tactics don't have the answer. Exercise

---

37 Ibid
38 Hirsch, Mark A., Erwin E. H. van Wegen, Mark A. Newman, and Patricia C. Heyn. 2018. "Exercise-Induced Increase In Brain-Derived Neurotrophic Factor In Human Parkinson's Disease: A Systematic Review And Meta-Analysis". Translational Neurodegeneration

is one of the most all-encompassing transformations you can do to positively impact your body.

So, if exercise is so good for your overall health, then what should one's exercise prescription be? Everyone is built a little differently and not everyone can perform the same activities. Some people prefer fishing rather than going to the gym, others prefer playing baseball than going on a run. The beauty of the exercise prescription is that there are many ways to get your weekly amount of exercise, as long as you remember a few key guidelines to what counts as physical activity.

The PAG recommends that healthy adults get 150 minutes of moderately intense exercise a week or seventy-five minutes of vigorous exercise a week[39]. Things like a brisk walk count for moderate activities, while going for a run would be counted as vigorous. As a general rule of thumb, if you're still able to hold a conversation while doing the activity it is moderate, but if it gets too difficult to talk, then you are most likely doing vigorous activities. During their weekly time for exercise, the PAG also suggests that adults participate in muscle strengthening activities at least twice a week to maintain musculoskeletal health as well. Here are the guidelines one more time in an easy-to-read format as part of the US government's, "move your way" campaign:

---

39 "Physical Activity Guidelines for Americans 2nd Edition". Health.Gov.

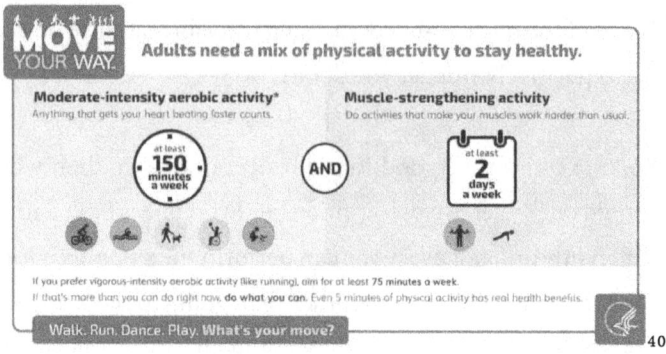

 Move Your Way.
Adults need a mix of physical activity to stay healthy.

Moderate-intensity aerobic activity*
Anything that gets your heart beating faster counts.

at least
150
minutes
a week

AND

Muscle-strengthening activity
Do activities that make your muscles work harder than usual.

at least
2
days
a week

If you prefer vigorous-intensity aerobic activity (like running), aim for at least 75 minutes a week.
If that's more than you can do right now, **do what you can.** Even 5 minutes of physical activity has real health benefits.

Walk. Run. Dance. Play. What's your move?

[40]

The guidelines for older adults are the same as those for adults eighteen and older. The difference is in the activities that older adults may elect to participate in. As you age, it becomes increasingly difficult to move around and exercise, especially if you haven't been doing it consistently since your youth. For this reason, the guidelines suggest that older adults do what they can and be "as active as possible" to gain as many benefits as possible[41].

Some may ask why 150 minutes a week? Why can't I do more or less? Well it's not that you can't do a different amount, but it's because at 150 minutes a week (or seventy-five minutes of vigorous activity) is where you receive the most benefits in regard to the amount of time you put in. It's easier to understand when examining the dose-response curve for weekly physical activity. [42]

---

40 Ibid
41 "Physical Activity Guidelines for Americans 2nd Edition". Health.Gov.
42 Ibid

Figure 2-1. Relationship of Moderate-to-Vigorous Physical Activity
to All-Cause Mortality

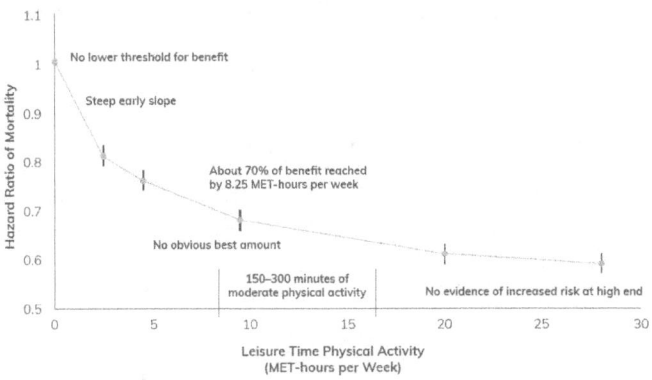

Source: Adapted from data found in Moore SC, Patel AV, Matthews CE. Leisure time physical activity of moderate to vigorous intensity and mortality: a large pooled cohort analysis. PLoS Med. 2012;9(11):e1001335. doi:10.1371/journal.pmed.1001335.

The chart above is from the 2018 Physical Activity Guidelines for Americans and shows the relationship between physical activity and your chances for death[43]. The slope of the graph is initially steep, which tells us that the greatest reduction in mortality risk comes from just by beginning to move around. The slope begins to slow down as you approach the 150-minute mark, so at that point you will receive almost as much health benefits as those people who go the extra mile and exceed their weekly requirements.

However, this shouldn't discourage you from going above and beyond the guidelines because, although not as pronounced, there is still extra benefit in being more active. The

---

43   "Physical Activity Guidelines for Americans 2nd Edition". Health.Gov.

point, however, is to show how bad being inactive is for you, and that by sitting around we increase our chance of death. Moving around literally helps to keep you alive.

For kids especially, depending on their age, things get slightly different. Since children are still developing, it is especially important for them to be more active to gain the developmental benefits that exercise can offer. These include not only physical benefits of ensuring strong bone and muscle growth, but it also helps with social and cognitive development[44]. The PAG lists its recommended amount of activity for children six to seventeen years old below:

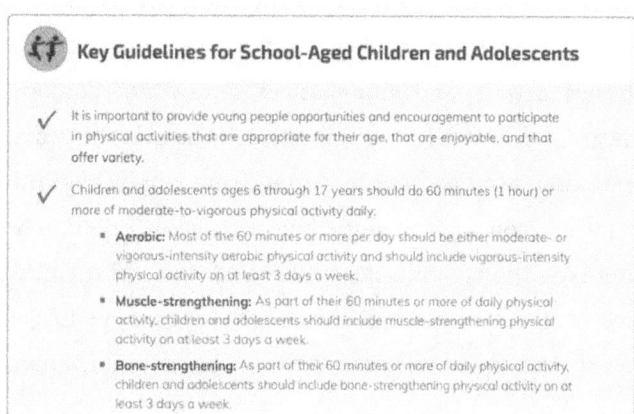

Key Guidelines for School-Aged Children and Adolescents

✓ It is important to provide young people opportunities and encouragement to participate in physical activities that are appropriate for their age, that are enjoyable, and that offer variety.

✓ Children and adolescents ages 6 through 17 years should do 60 minutes (1 hour) or more of moderate-to-vigorous physical activity daily:

- **Aerobic:** Most of the 60 minutes or more per day should be either moderate- or vigorous-intensity aerobic physical activity and should include vigorous-intensity physical activity on at least 3 days a week.

- **Muscle-strengthening:** As part of their 60 minutes or more of daily physical activity, children and adolescents should include muscle-strengthening physical activity on at least 3 days a week.

- **Bone-strengthening:** As part of their 60 minutes or more of daily physical activity, children and adolescents should include bone-strengthening physical activity on at least 3 days a week.

[45]

---

44 Ibid
45 "Physical Activity Guidelines for Americans 2nd Edition"

For kids younger than six, the health officials encourage them to be as active as possible throughout the day. This will help enhance their growth and development throughout their younger years[46]. For this reason, schools should be encouraged to plan out activities that include some sort of physical activity throughout the day. Here are the recommendations for preschool children:[47]

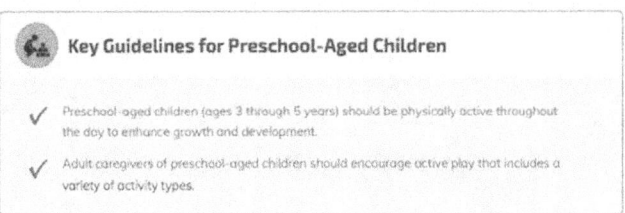

Key Guidelines for Preschool-Aged Children

✓ Preschool-aged children (ages 3 through 5 years) should be physically active throughout the day to enhance growth and development.

✓ Adult caregivers of preschool-aged children should encourage active play that includes a variety of activity types.

WHAT COUNTS AS EXERCISE?

A huge misconception is that you need to go to the gym or pick up a sport to be physically active. Unlimited options exist as to what constitutes as physical activity, here are some examples:

---

46 Ibid
47 Ibid

Table 3-1. Examples of Aerobic, Muscle-, and Bone-Strengthening Physical Activities for Children and Adolescents

Type of Physical Activity	Preschool-Aged Children	School-Aged Children	Adolescents
Moderate-intensity aerobic	• Games such as tag or follow the leader • Playing on a playground • Tricycle or bicycle riding • Walking, running, skipping, jumping, dancing • Swimming • Playing games that require catching, throwing, and kicking • Gymnastics or tumbling	• Brisk walking • Bicycle riding • Active recreation, such as hiking, riding a scooter without a motor, swimming • Playing games that require catching and throwing, such as baseball and softball	• Brisk walking • Bicycle riding • Active recreation, such as kayaking, hiking, swimming • Playing games that require catching and throwing, such as baseball and softball • House and yard work, such as sweeping or pushing a lawn mower • Some video games that include continuous movement
Vigorous-intensity aerobic	• Games such as tag or follow the leader • Playing on a playground • Tricycle or bicycle riding • Walking, running, skipping, jumping, dancing • Swimming • Playing games that require catching, throwing, and kicking • Gymnastics or tumbling	• Running • Bicycle riding • Active games involving running and chasing, such as tag or flag football • Jumping rope • Cross-country skiing • Sports such as soccer, basketball, swimming, tennis • Martial arts • Vigorous dancing	• Running • Bicycle riding • Active games involving running and chasing, such as flag football • Jumping rope • Cross-country skiing • Sports such as soccer, basketball, swimming, tennis • Martial arts • Vigorous dancing

48

---

48 "Physical Activity Guidelines for Americans 2nd Edition". Health.Gov.

Table 4-1. Examples of Different Aerobic Physical Activities and Intensities, Based on Absolute Intensity

Moderate-Intensity Activities

- Walking briskly (2.5 miles per hour or faster)
- Recreational swimming
- Bicycling slower than 10 miles per hour on level terrain
- Tennis (doubles)
- Active forms of yoga (for example, Vinyasa or power yoga)
- Ballroom or line dancing
- General yard work and home repair work
- Exercise classes like water aerobics

Vigorous-Intensity Activities

- Jogging or running
- Swimming laps
- Tennis (singles)
- Vigorous dancing
- Bicycling faster than 10 miles per hour
- Jumping rope
- Heavy yard work (digging or shoveling, with heart rate increases)
- Hiking uphill or with a heavy backpack
- High-intensity interval training (HIIT)
- Exercise classes like vigorous step aerobics or kickboxing

49

As long as an activity gets your whole body moving, then a general rule of thumb is that you can count it towards your totals. By achieving the recommended weekly exercise totals, your risk for diseases such as cardiovascular diseases, cancer, hypertension, diabetes, and many others diminish, and you will also see improvements in your sleep, focus, mood, bone and muscle health, and overall function[50]. With all these benefits, it's important to start making physical activity something more than merely a suggestion, but instead a normal part of life. I want each of us to begin to

---

49 "Physical Activity Guidelines for Americans 2nd Edition". Health.Gov.
50 Ibid

see how exercise is no different than taking our daily pills for what ails us. If we miss a pill, it could greatly affect our life. Similarly, if we don't include physical activity, it could greatly affect our lives.

Think back to the last time you were in a doctor's office. Generally, the nurse comes in to take your vitals and maybe ask you a few questions such as, "Do you smoke?" or "How have you been sleeping?" Less often do they ask you about your physical activity levels and even when they do, it is in a nonspecific manner like "have you been exercising?"

Dr. Elizabeth Joy, former president for the American College of Sports Medicine, believes that this is a major problem we face in the healthcare profession. In an interview, she gives the example that you would never just look at a person and assume their blood pressure or heart rate, but instead you have tools to measure the exact number[51]. The same thing should go for physical activity because you can't just look at someone who is skinny and assume they get enough exercise; how would you know if you don't ask?

She suggests adding a few questions to the questionnaire that you fill out at your doctor's office, such as how many days a week are you physically active, and for how long do you

51   "VIDEO REPLAY: Dr. Liz Joy Gives 2019 Blyth Lecture | Department Of Exercise And Sport Science". 2019. Exss.Unc.Edu

generally participate in these activities? She also wants to know the types of activities patients participate in to see if they are hitting the recommended amount of weekly exercise[52].

Knowing whether patients are reaching recommended values is important because it gives healthcare professionals better insight to a patient's potential risk factors. Just looking at someone and judging their fitness based on their weight won't cut it, as studies have shown that cardiovascular fitness is a better predictor of disease risk and all-cause mortality than obesity, smoking, or being diabetic. In fact, in studies done on a cohort of Type II diabetics, data showed that individuals who were obese, but still met weekly physical activity guidelines, were at less risk for all-cause mortality than normal-weight individuals that didn't meet the guidelines[53].

The importance of physical activity as a health marker should be something that is incorporated in every doctor's office in America due to how valuable of a tool it can be. This will also allow healthcare professionals to take better care of patients and give them suggestions on how to improve their levels of physical activity in a safe manner. Doctors can suggest walking programs, group fitness classes, or even activities

---

52 Ibid
53 Church et al. 2003. "Exercise Capacity And Body Composition As Predictors Of Mortality Among Men With Diabetes". Diabetes Care 27 (1): 83-88. American Diabetes Association

at home such as gardening or dancing to increase exercise levels, which will in turn help reduce their risk of various conditions. With this knowledge, healthcare professionals can begin giving their exercise prescriptions, which will be custom fit to each patient's needs.

The more that exercise gets incorporated into the healthcare system, the more people will become conscious of the importance of exercise for your health. If exercise levels were to increase and awareness rises, we could see more people reaching their weekly goals for physical activity, and see a dramatic increase in their quality of life. Countless healthcare dollars will be saved relieving the financial burden on so many people in the nation, as well as the stress it places on our government agencies. The incorporation of physical activity in all aspects of life is the key to a healthy population.

CHAPTER 2

THE SITTING DISEASE

———

One of the biggest contributors to the health crisis that we face is not what you would you think. If I asked you what activity you thought would be the most destructive to a person's health, you would probably rattle off a list that included smoking cigarettes or eating too much fast food, but recent studies suggest that we have to be wary of a new threat. What's worse is that this threat requires no energy to accomplish and is steadily on the rise due to our continuous push to make life effortless and more convenient. Although it may seem harmless, the threat to our health is none other than just sitting down.

Some media outlets say that sitting has now become the new smoking, which makes sense when you remember so many people don't know the negative effects it can have on their overall health. Nothing is wrong with sitting down to relax during your lunch break, but what is alarming is the amount of time Americans are spending sitting down throughout the day. The average person spends about 7.7 hours a day sitting or being sedentary; that's 55 percent of their monitored time being awake[54].

To understand the implications of this, we need to first understand what is going on inside the body when you sit. Exercise physiologists use the metabolic equivalence of task (M.E.T.), which is an objective measure of how much energy a person is expanding for a particular task[55]. The greater the M.E.T. value, the more energy that activity requires, so for example, things like jumping rope expend 12.3 M.E.T. on average, and humans have even reaching values higher than twenty-three when sprinting at higher speeds[56]. On the other end of the spectrum, sedentary behavior is defined as exerting 1.5 or less M.E.T during activity.

Things such as watching the game on TV while in the recliner, sitting and typing on your computer during work, or sitting

---

54 Matthews et al. 2008. "Amount Of Time Spent In Sedentary Behaviors In The United States, 2003-2004". American Journal Of Epidemiology

55 Jetté M, et al. 2019. "Metabolic Equivalents (METS) In Exercise Testing, Exercise Prescription, And Evaluation Of Functional Capacity. - Pubmed - NCBI

56 McCall, Pete. 2017. "5 Things To Know About Metabolic Equivalents". Acefitness.Org.

through a class lecture are all things that constitute as low M.E.T. behaviors. While some things like watching the game are optional, other activities are affiliated with work or school are not, so it's not like we have a choice, but after learning about some of the dangers involved with sitting, you might reconsider how you go about your mandatory daily activities.

So, what's the big deal with sitting down? Why is it so dangerous? Shouldn't you be able to watch your favorite team play after a long day of work and be unbothered by the thought that you could potentially be hurting your health?

To help answer these questions we can look to a study run by the National Cancer Institute in 2015. They examined over 200,000 individuals and asked them questions about their TV viewing habits and health history. They wanted to see if increasing the number of hours spent sitting increased your chances for some of the leading causes of death such as cancer, heart diseases, and diabetes.

The retrospective study revealed that just by watching TV for an additional two hours a day you increase your chance of death from conditions like cancer and heart disease among others[57].

---

57   Keadle et al. 2015. "Causes Of Death Associated With Prolonged TV Viewing". American Journal Of Preventive Medicine

Again, there is no problem with well-deserved rest and relaxation, but it needs to be earned. However, the unfortunate truth is that many of us don't compensate our hours spent sitting with some type of physical activity to justify watching an extra episode of Netflix. Just because you're being productive in the workplace doesn't mean you are being productive for your body, and understanding that is essential if we are to make a change in our daily lives.

In a lot of ways, the human body is just like a car. Many vehicles, if left sitting in the garage for too long, will either not be able to start or have some issue due to the lack of use. The human body is the same way because the less you use parts of the body, the more those muscles will atrophy, or break down, to conserve the energy that is no longer being used. The phrase, "use it or lose it" is more accurate than people think, as the body is cruel and has no problem starving the unused muscle, so that way nutrients can serve other parts of the body that need it.

Sitting is the fourth leading factor for global mortality, accounting for 3.2 million deaths a year that all have some type of association with being sedentary[58]. The sad news is that many of these cases and conditions can be prevented or at least mitigated just by exercising or getting into any new

---

58 HEALTH, PHYSICAL. 2010. "PHYSICAL ACTIVITY FOR HEALTH". World Health Organization.

hobby that doesn't include sitting down. In a very literal way, moving around can save your life.

It is also estimated that "about half of American adults—117 million people—have one or more preventable chronic diseases."[59] The key word here is preventable, as the chance for acquiring a lot of these are diseases can be decreased just by meeting the weekly guidelines for exercise discussed in the previous chapter (generally 150 minutes a week of moderate exercise). Some of these preventable conditions include cardiovascular disease, type II diabetes, and various types of cancer[60].

Sedentary behavior also increases your likelihood for obesity. Obesity in itself already complicates our health, putting us at greater risk for all the previous conditions mentioned, so being sedentary can be a potential "double whammy" in terms of the disadvantages for our health.

The physical activity guidelines scientific report also shows the direct link between the amount of time spent sitting and the cause of mortality. In an analysis of twenty different studies, researchers found that people who are more sedentary, and don't meet weekly guidelines for activity, have a hazard

59 "Nutrition And Health Are Closely Related - 2015-2020 Dietary Guidelines - Health.Gov". 2019. Health.Gov

60 "Physical Activity Guidelines for Americans 2nd Edition". Health.Gov.

ratio of 1.22 compared to their fitter counterparts[61]. This means that less active individuals are 22 percent more likely to die just based on their sedentary behavior. This means the more you sit, the more likely you are to face a life-threatening disease that can rob you of your life early. Although a gloomy realization, there is still hope, as even a little bit of moving around can go a long way.

A common misconception is that little amounts of physical activity doesn't really do much for your health. Even early scientists thought that for you to receive any benefit, you had to be active for at least ten minutes. Thankfully, new research has provided evidence to show that being physically active can have immediate effects, which include reducing things such as decreasing anxiety and blood pressure.[62]

In fact, you don't even have to be moving to be benefiting your body, as even just standing can help benefit bone health and posture, fight against diseases like osteoarthritis, and help prevent risk from cardiovascular disease by helping improve circulation throughout your body[63]. Improving your circulation increases blood supply to the brain, which helps improve focus, which is one of the biggest reasons why

61   "Scientific Report" 2019. Health.Gov.
62   "Physical Activity Guidelines for Americans 2nd Edition". Health.Gov.
63   "The Facts Behind 'Sitting Disease' And Living Sedentary | Just-stand.Org".

many offices and schools are starting to introduce things like stand-up desks.

A recent study was conducted seeing the effect of introducing stand-up desks in a workplace. One hundred and thirty-seven employees working in Australia had fourteen biological markers, including insulin, blood pressure, and body composition, measured throughout a period of a year to help calculate their risk for cardiometabolic diseases after transitioning from sitting desks to standing desks. When comparing the results to the beginning of the study, researchers found that cardiometabolic risk was decreased in a majority of the cohort[64].

Finally, standing allows fat burning enzymes in the body to stay activated, allowing you to burn more calories and reduce the risk of becoming obese, which can further increase your risk for all the diseases associated with obesity. Although it may seem discouraging that just by sitting, we run the risk of increasing our chances to acquire a life-threatening disease, but we can rest easy knowing that by putting in a little bit of effort, we can mitigate the degenerative effects of leading a sedentary lifestyle.

---

64 Gao et al. 2018. "Economic Evaluation Of A Randomized Controlled Trial Of An Intervention To Reduce Office Workers' Sitting Time: The "Stand Up Victoria" Trial". Scandinavian Journal Of Work, Environment & Health

Aside from the many health concerns that should hopefully make us wary of the "sitting disease," there is also a large financial component that accompanies the many reasons why you should be physically active. It is estimated that about 117 billion dollars are spent in healthcare costs annually due to inadequate physical activity levels[65]. Yes, that's 117 billion in costs that could have been saved. That's enough to give every man, woman, and child in the whole country of Canada $3,250[66].

While a lot of this money comes in the form of mandatory healthcare payments, this money can instead be allocated to better serving those who pay into the system by providing things such as high-quality facilities and up-to-date medical equipment. This money can also be cycled back to communities that can't afford certain services. For example, providing free walk-in clinics in poverty-stricken areas or free classes about various topics such as mental and sexual health to make sure communities are properly educated on topics that can keep them healthy for the long term.

With the new evidence that shows the issues associated with sitting, something must be done to combat these problems.

---

65 "Inadequate Physical Activity and Health Care Expenditures in the United States" 2019. Cdc.Gov.
66 "How Much Is 117 Billion? (How Much Is 117,000,000,000?)". 2019. Researchmaniacs.Com

The only way to win the fight against inactivity is through education. If people don't know the negative effects of being sedentary, then why would they think about stopping? To truly make a difference in their lives, they have to genuinely care and understand how their actions, or in this case inactions, can hurt them. This starts at a young age, as we need to start educating the youth of the importance of physical activity so that they can carry this knowledge and learn to apply it over time. The strongest habits are built during childhood so we have to start early.

CHAPTER 3

MOTIVATED MUSCLE

———

One of the most well-known benefits of exercise has to be that it can make you bigger and stronger. For years, people have been lifting weights to get bigger arms and "shredded" abs, all with the hope of achieving the coveted "Arnold" physique that many weightlifters strive for. In fact, there is no other safe way to allow your body to transform itself into a stronger version of itself unless you do some type of exercise. For this reason, millions of people get to the gym right before spring break to make sure they're ready for those pictures on the beach.

Of course, there is nothing wrong with this mentality, as whatever motivates you to become more physically active can't be a bad thing. However, eventually people begin to care less about their appearance to others and begin to slip back into sedentary habits. Combine the lack of motivation with obligations from work or school and the fact is that finding time for exercise can be tricky. But by adjusting your motives for why you exercise in the first place, you can learn to make time.

Self Determination Theory (SDT) is a psychological framework for human motivation and personality. Included in this framework is a spectrum showing different types of motivations ranging from extrinsic, or external motivators, to intrinsic, or internal motivators. Below you can see the different motivational types:

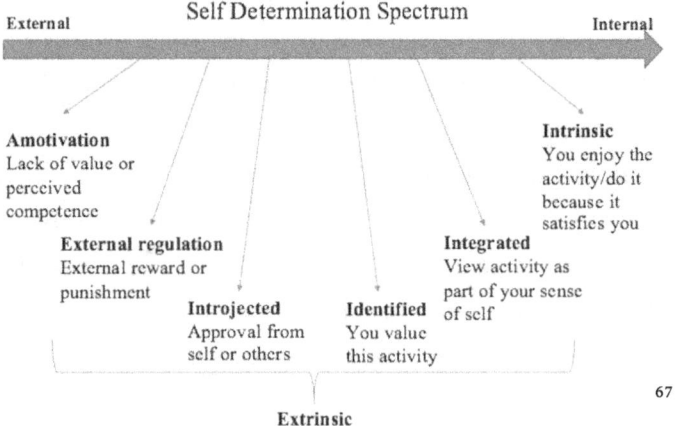

67   EL, Ryan. 2019. "Self-Determination Theory And The Facilitation Of Intrinsic Motivation, Social Development, And Well-Being. - Pubmed - NCBI

By looking at the chart you can see that the more internal reasons for motivation are toward the intrinsic side of the spectrum, which makes sense as the more internal the motivators in your life are, the more likely you are to do it. For example, people who find an exercise they like to do, let's say going hiking, are more likely to hike on their own accord. The approval of others is an extrinsic motivator, which is why working out to impress people on vacation may be hard to stick to once you get back from vacation. To keep it simple, the more you do something simply because you like it, the more likely you are to make it a habit.

A study done by the University of Western Ontario in Canada wanted to put this theory to the test and recruited over 1000 "regular exercisers" to participate, and answer questions about their physical activity levels and different motivational factors they had for exercising. They found that those who exercised because of more internal motivators got more moderate to vigorous weekly activity than those who said they did it for external reasons. They also found that more internal motivators were important contributors to the duration and frequency of exercise, not just intensity[68].

---

68 Duncan et al. 2010. "Exercise Motivation: A Cross-Sectional Analysis Examining Its Relationships With Frequency, Intensity, And Duration Of Exercise". International Journal Of Behavioral Nutrition And Physical Activity

This is why we must build different motivations to stay active and always make long-term health our goal. Just like with the cardiovascular and respiratory benefits of physical activity, there are plenty of reasons to continue to be physically active past your prime in a swimsuit. Training your musculoskeletal system allows you to be more functional in all other facets of life. Bone and muscle strengthening activities help preserve bones and joints, build muscle mass, and allow you the freedom to do the hobbies you love.

Bone health is very important as you get older and when you're first starting to grow. Older adults are at a higher risk for developing conditions like osteoarthritis because as you age your bone density begins to decrease as bones lose important minerals like calcium. This is especially seen in women going through menopause, as one of the side effects is also loss of bone density, leading to osteoporosis. Exercising regularly helps reduce the chance for those diseases and helps ensure that older adults are able to stay active for a longer period of their life.

For those already diagnosed with osteoarthritis, exercise can become painful and many people worry that it will only make their condition worse. This causes people to be less physically active, which can actually end up being more detrimental, as doing so increases your risk for heart disease and type II diabetes. Knowing the horrible downward spiral that this disease can cause, researchers studied the effect of walking on over 1,700 individuals with osteoarthritis to see if there were dangers associated with exercising with the condition. Specifically, their study looked at the effect walking had on knee pain and health and their results proved the opposite of what people might have expected.

Tracking the subjects for a week, they measured the effects that walking had on pain in their knees, functionality, and surveyed their daily exercise history. The researchers found that for every additional 1,000 steps they took a day, they had their risk for functional limitation decreased by 16 percent to 18 percent. They also found no evidence that walking up to 10,000 steps a day would worsen their condition[69].

As you become older, muscle atrophy also increases, making everyday tasks that you once deemed as easy become increasingly difficult. Before that time comes, it is easy to take things such as doing the dishes and going up the stairs for granted, but just like in the case with my family, diseases can accelerate the process of deterioration and something you used to think wasn't strenuous can eventually feel like a whole body workout.

---

69 White et al. 2014. "Daily Walking And The Risk Of Incident Functional Limitation In Knee Osteoarthritis: An Observational Study". Arthritis Care & Research

Finally, as you get older your risks for falling increase as well. Every year, one in four older adults suffer from a fall sending someone to the hospital every eleven seconds[70]. Unfortunately, every nineteen minutes an older adult also passes away due to a fall[71]. These statistics show a scary reality when it comes to aging and besides making sure your home is safe of potential hazards, one of the only things that we are able to do to prevent injury due to falls is to be physically active. By exercising more and meeting guidelines for movement you increase your balance, coordination, and your bone strength, helping prevent injury during a fall or allowing you to catch yourself even when you trip[72].

The government and its citizens can also save a great deal of money by training their bodies to avoid falls, as injuries due to falling cost the US 50 billion dollars in 2016, 75 percent of which was covered by Medicare and Medicaid.[73] These funds can be reallocated to better help those on disability or those who have a lower income. All it would take would be for all of us to care for our bodies by becoming more active, and we could reduce the amount of injuries due to falls dramatically.

70 "Fall Prevention Stats". 2019. Ncoa.Org
71 Ibid
72 "Physical Activity Guidelines for Americans 2nd Edition". Health.Gov.
73 "Important Facts About Falls | Home And Recreational Safety | CDC Injury Center". 2019. Cdc.Gov

The risk for losing your freedom to any of these conditions can be decreased just by getting your weekly amount of exercise, but what happens if you're already in bad shape? Pasquale Brocco a.k.a. "possible Pat" would tell you that no matter the odds, it is not too late to make a change. Pat once weighed in at 605 pounds and doctors warned him that he could die if he didn't make a change in his life[74]. The turning point in his life came when Pat lost a bet where he had to do fifty push-ups; he couldn't even do one. With the doctor's words still resonating with him, he knew he had to do something before he was struck with a terrible disease.

He decided to throw everything in his fridge out and start over, but he didn't just stop there. To incentivize doing exercise he decided he would walk to the nearest Walmart located a mile away to get food for every meal. Three meals a day would mean he would walk about six miles every day, and in a year and a half he had lost 200 pounds.

He remembers that he couldn't even go to the gym because he couldn't fit on the machines, but now that he has been able to go to the gym he fell in love and now has aspirations of being a bodybuilder. Pat is down over 330 pounds and counting, proving that no matter how bad your fitness level is when you start, it's never too late to switch paths and take

---

74 "About". 2019. Possible Pat.

ownership of your life. More importantly, he said that he wanted to "set an example for his son, so that he can grow up and be possible Pat too."[75] Pat didn't want his son to go through the same bullying that he did and he knew that these lifestyle habits are built in a person's younger years, just like they had for him.

We often take this for granted as children, but whatever you do to your body will carry with you into adulthood, as those who do not meet the physical activity guidelines for exercise are at higher risks for diseases such as osteoporosis, arthritis, and tendonitis, which can cripple your quality of life and ability to enjoy your favorite activities[76].

The physical activity guidelines suggest that children participate in bone and muscle strengthening activities at least three times a week. Doing this is essential for not only building habits, but also helping catalyze healthy bone and muscle development as the body matures.[77] Doing things such as running, jumping, playing on monkey bars, and all other types of things are considered activities that help bone and muscle development, even though they are activities not traditionally viewed as "weightlifting." Doing anything that involves using your

75   "About". 2019. Possible Pat.
76   "Physical Activity Guidelines for Americans 2nd Edition". Health.Gov
77   Ibid

body weight for resistance is a great way to train your muscles, and what's even better is that you don't need a gym membership to start.

Achieving your recommended amount of weekly exercise can help develop bone density and muscle mass in the youth and promote healthy growth for an individual, which is essential when someone is young. Strengthening the bones and muscles in your body will also help you improve balance, coordination, functionality, and overall strength to carry you through your life, literally![78]

Sometimes, to understand the transformative power of exercise, we need to look at extreme examples. Most people would think that being born with a physical disability, especially one like dwarfism, means that having a dream of being strong and physically fit is impossible.

Aditya Dev is a perfect example of someone who proves that big things can come in small sizes. Better known by his nickname "Romeo" he is known around the world as the world's smallest bodybuilder, but his journey to his coveted title has been anything but easy. He was born in Phagwara, India with a condition called primordial dwarfism and only weighed one and a half pounds at birth, only one-fifth the size of a

---

78 Ibid

normal newborn. Doctors gave him little chance to live, but he overcame the odds and survived.[79]

Some people in Indian culture view children born with dwarfism as a sign that their family has been cursed for deeds in their past life. So, growing up, Romeo faced discrimination from onlookers whether at school, on the street, or at the gym.

Romeo never let them get to him and was determined to live the life that he wanted to. He saw the growing trend of bodybuilding in India and looked no further for a new hobby, despite being the complete opposite of people such as Arnold Schwarzenegger, Ronnie Coleman, and other famous bodybuilders.

He said it all started when his friend told him that he should go train with him. Romeo remembers telling him that he couldn't, "because my body wouldn't develop," due to his disease, but his friend urged him to trust him and just try it out anyway. He assured him that they would start slow, but that he would still feel the difference. His friend was right, as Romeo finally began to see muscle forming saying that, "it finally began to set. The muscle just became like stone. It set like stone."

---

79 "The World's Smallest Muscleman (Extraordinary People Documentary) | Real Stories". 2019. Youtube

Amazed by the results of his new lifestyle, he never looked back, working out multiple times a week with famous people like Avtar, Indian reality TV show winner, and Jason "Wee Man" Acuña, star of hit TV show *Jackass.*

In fact, every day he has people coming to ask him his story, drawing inspiration from it and even asking for a picture before resuming their own workouts. In February 2008, his hard work was rewarded as the Indian equivalent of the Guinness Book of World Records, the Limca Book of Records, had given him the title of World's Smallest Bodybuilder, something Romeo was delighted to receive.

His sister says that she, "thinks that he has slapped all the people in the face who said that he couldn't do anything. He showed them he can do everything." His family now says that despite their culture, they believe that, "he is a miracle from God," and believe in his talents to go on and pursue his dreams.[80]

It's always inspiring to see someone accomplishing their goals, even when the cards seemed to be against them. Not only did he use exercise to follow his dreams, but he also reaped the benefits of being active to help improve his quality of life. Lifting and running around gave him the confidence

---

80 "The World's Smallest Muscleman (Extraordinary People Documentary) | Real Stories". 2019. Youtube

that helped maintain his mental health, as well as improve cardiovascular function, and prevent or at least mitigate the effects of blood vessel abnormalities that you might have generally seen with patients who have primordial dwarfism[81]. It also increased his strength and muscle function allowing him to curl close to five pounds in each arm, which now allows him to perform activities for daily living (ADLs) that he wasn't able to do before such as grabbing heavy groceries or moving things around the house.

Now, although an extreme example, this is a perfect way to show how exercise can literally change your life and mind-set instantly. If someone who is so small that he showers in a sink and can find the motivation to go to the gym, then we should be able to go for a run, or play basketball or do whatever type of activity we prefer to improve our immediate and long-term health. His ability to use exercise to breed confidence in himself to achieve his other goals as well should be something we all draw inspiration from, and should hopefully remind us that there are others who are busier and less fortunate that still find the time to take care of their bodies.

---

81   Reference, Genetics. 2019. "MOPDII". Genetics Home Reference

CHAPTER 4

A HEALTHY HEART

———

Although perceived as common knowledge now, little was known about the effect of exercise on the heart in the early parts of the 1900s, even though philosophers such as Hippocrates have previously noted the holistic benefit that exercise has on the whole body[82]. Some people in the scientific community even denounced some of the earlier findings making studying the topic unfruitful and career ending at times.[83] Thankfully, there were still researchers who believed in their work and dismissed the negative opinions of others and continued to find the evidence to prove the benefits that exercise can have on the whole cardiovascular system.

---

82 Tipton, Charles M. 2014. "The History Of "Exercise Is Medicine" In Ancient Civilizations". Advances In Physiology Education

83 Ibid

One of these researchers was Lawrence Henderson who is more well known for his contributions to chemistry than the body's response to physical activity, also known as exercise physiology. Henderson was a graduate of Harvard College and Harvard Medical School, eventually going on to teach and do research at Harvard later on. He is most famously known for being of the mind to create the Henderson-Hasselbalch equation, which helps calculate the pH in different solutions and pH equilibrium in acid-based solutions.[84]

As someone who hated chemistry throughout high school and college, especially any questions having to do with this equation specifically, I'll be the first to tell you that calculating pH change is not that exciting, but in the chemistry world that equation was a big deal. Not only because it gave professors more material to ask questions on, but more importantly it allowed scientists to calculate the effect of pH change in the body and how that can influence different reactions, including how proteins are made. This would also be essential for the pharmaceutical industry to manufacture drugs that would respond well to pH changes and ensure that they were still effective.[85]

---

84 "Biographical Memoir of Lawrence Henderson" 2019. Nasonline.Org.
85 Mehta, Akul. 2014. "Applications And Example Problems Using Henderson–Hasselbalch Equation | Analytical Chemistry | Pharmaxchange.Info". Pharmaxchange.Info

After his work in chemistry, he turned his focus to writing and also began to work with physiology, which is the study of how all of the systems of the body operate individually and in unison. He grew a liking to this new study and, using his previous success, he founded the Harvard Fatigue Laboratory which is viewed as the first physiology lab ever made.[86] This was huge because it established exercise physiology as a discipline and opened the door for others to begin researching the topic.

Over the time the lab was in existence, the lab published many pioneering studies that were the first of its kind, many to do with the cardiovascular system. They tested things such as blood pressure, red blood cell count, and different molecule concentrations such as oxygen and lactic acid in the blood. One study they published found that exercising can increase blood oxygen capacity by up to 10 percent helping individuals in energy production, while another study found that exercising can help increase red blood cell (RBC) count by 10 percent and leukocyte count, which deals with immunity, by 200 to 300%. This showed the beneficial effects on immunity and energy efficiency that physical activity has on the body, the first studies of their kind.[87]

---

86 "Biographical Memoir of Lawrence Henderson" 2019. Nasonline.Org.
87 "History Of Exercise Physiology: Harvard Fatigue Laboratory Influential In Promoting Exercise Physiology Research". 2019. Human-Kinetics

Henderson died in 1942 and shortly after so did the Fatigue Laboratory, but his work served as a major catalyst for exercise physiology promotion, bringing credibility to the discipline and inspiring others to continue his work, including a man named Thomas Cureton. Cureton was a professor at the University of Illinois and one of the main people to push the physical activity intuitive to fruition through his use of academic evidence to back his findings. Nicknamed the "father of physical fitness" he was also founder of the Physical Fitness Research Laboratory where he conducted his groundbreaking research on everyone from youth swimmers to Olympic athletes.[88]

In the 1960s, he began his work on cardiovascular function finding that, "exercise helped support heart longevity and protected against degenerative diseases" that affect the cardiovascular system. He was also one of the first to note the training effects that exercise can have on the cardiovascular system. One study he did saw nineteen men split into two groups, one that worked out two days a week and one that worked out four days a week. At the end of the intervention weight, a study of nineteen men compared body composition and cardiovascular function between the groups and, as he expected, subjects who exercised more not only lost more

88   JW, Berryman. 2019. "Thomas K. Cureton, Jr.: Pioneer Researcher, Proselytizer, And Proponent For Physical Fitness. - Pubmed - NCBI

weight, but had also performed better cardiovascularly. This was one of the first studies done of its kind, as it showed the performance benefits that exercise can have as well. He not only taught about the research that he conducted, but he lived it, winning five gold medals at the first National Masters Swimming Championship at the age of 72, all in the effort to protect his heart for the long term.[89]

Another pioneer in exercise research was United States veteran Dr. Kenneth Cooper, also known as the "father of aerobics." He was a flight surgeon and the director of the aerospace medical laboratory serving the Air Force for thirteen years. Cooper was a frequent exerciser and had noticed the improvement it had on his overall health and believed that everyone could benefit from it. While serving in the military, he also began to find interest in preventative medicine research. Just by noting changes in his own body, he hypothesized that getting your heart rate up was directly correlated with improvements in your heart health. So, he began his studies and examined the effect of this type of physical activity that he called "aerobic exercise" on around 5,000 members of the Air Force, and to his excitement his results helped confirm what he thought for so long.[90]

---

89 "Thomas K. Cureton Jr.; Physical Fitness Expert, 91". 2019. Nytimes.Com.

90 "Cooper Aerobics". 2019. Cooperaerobics.Com

He found that exercise strengthened the muscles that were controlling inhalation and exhalation, and also helped strengthen the muscles in the heart. Both of these improvements resulted in an overall decrease in resting blood pressure. He also predicted that exercise increased your red blood cell count, meaning that it helped the blood become a better carrier of oxygen just like the researchers at the Harvard Fatigue Laboratory had found as well.

Using these results, he also derived a test which was designed to assess cardiovascular fitness. The object of the exam was to have a participant run as far as possible at an even pace in twelve minutes. Using the distance, he came up with a formula that could estimate your VO2 max, which is just a measure of how well your body can use oxygen during physical activity.

Cooper's finding showed that exercise not only benefits those who do it, but also how beneficial it could be as a measure for health and fitness. The military eventually adopted this test to examine their incoming cadets, it became so popular due to its usefulness that it became a standard measure in the fitness industry and for the public in general, formally becoming known as the Cooper Test.

The success of his results also aided Cooper in starting his not-for-profit organization called Cooper Aerobics in 1970, which aimed to help further research and awareness on the positive effects of aerobic exercise. Cooper also practiced what he preached as he generally never missed more than, "five consecutive days in getting some type of aerobic exercise."[91] He credits this consistency to be the reason for his fitness level at an older age saying, "we do not stop exercising because we get old; we get old because we stop exercising."

Later on, more researchers continued to find proof that would back his findings, proving the validity of his work. In many ways he was partially responsible for opening up this field of exercise research and helping it get to where it is now. He, along with all these other pioneers, gave the voice that exercise physiology needed to finally make it to the public realm.

Cooper may have also been the first person to start a national exercise fad as a combination from the notoriety of the test along with the implications of the results of his experiments made people want to receive these benefits as well. Before long, the aerobic exercise trend swept the nation and millions began to walk, jog, or do anything that would get their heart rates up to perform better and add years to their lives[92].

Thankfully, these research pioneers have done the hard work for us and we now have a good understanding of how the

---

91 "Cooper Aerobics". 2019. Cooperaerobics.Com
92 Ibid

circulatory system is mapped out. The cardiovascular system is made up of your heart, and all the blood vessels and blood that circulates through your arteries, capillaries, and veins. Their jobs are to transport oxygen and other molecules throughout the body to aid essential systems in manufacturing energy that can be used for the rest of the body. The cells that help in oxygen transport are called red blood cells (RBC), but there are also other types of cells, called white blood cells (WBC), whose jobs are to protect the body from foreign invaders that can cause diseases. These WBCs are one of the most important components to our body's immunity, so it makes sense that if our cardiovascular system isn't properly taken care of, then our immunity can also suffer.[93]

One would think that since WBCs protect us from disease that the more there are, the better we are protected, but the immune system is more complicated than that. Having a low WBC count is definitely a bad thing and can decrease your ability to fight diseases, but having an elevated WBC count can also be dangerous, as it is a marker of increased risk to coronary heart disease and death. It can be caused by a number of things, such as an infection, stress, thyroid problems, or inflammation, just to name a few.[94]

93 " What Are White Blood Cells? - Health Encyclopedia - University Of Rochester Medical Center ". 2019. Urmc.Rochester.Edu
94 "High White Blood Cell Count Causes". 2019. Mayo Clinic.

Medications are often prescribed for these problems, but one holistic medication that often goes unprescribed is exercise. A study published in the Public Library of Science examined data from 390 overweight postmenopausal women to see the effects different exercise interventions would have on their WBC. They divided the women into three groups, prescribing a different amount of exercise to each. After six months, the results showed that those individuals who were placed in the group that exercised more had a lower WBC count than the rest of the cohort.[95]

Besides helping to regulate blood cell count, exercise can also be beneficial to other parts of the cardiovascular system. The heart itself is a muscle, so just like with all the other muscles in our body, it is essential that we keep it functioning properly by giving it the right amount of exercise.

If you have ever taken a health class in middle school, the teacher most likely talked about how aerobic exercise is good for the heart, but very rarely would they explain why. There are many reasons, but some include combatting things like an increase in heart rate, blood pressure, and body fat, that can all result for being too inactive. An increase in any of these measurements put more stress on the heart, making it

---

95 Johannsen et al. 2012. "Effect Of Different Doses Of Aerobic Exercise On Total White Blood Cell (WBC) And WBC Subfraction Number In Postmenopausal Women: Results From DREW". Plos ONE 7

work even harder to pump all the blood through your body. The harder the heart must work, the greater the risk for cardiovascular diseases such as things like hypertension to more life-threatening ones such as stroke and heart disease.[96]

In fact, these conditions are two of the top five reasons for death in America.[97] To help avoid ever dealing with a deadly cardiovascular disease, we need to make sure we are getting sufficient weekly aerobic exercise. Not only will we help keep our blood pressure and other cardiovascular markers at a healthy level, but we also gain the freedom to go on a walk with our family, or be able to hike up our favorite trail without having to stop frequently. Having a healthy heart is one of the most important aspects of keeping control over your life, that way being out of breath will never stop you.

---

96 "Physical Inactivity And Cardiovascular Disease". 2019. Health. Ny.Gov.
97 "12 Leading Causes Of Death In The United States". 2019. Healthline.

CHAPTER 5

JUST BREATHE

———

Take a slow deep breath.

Feel the air as it rushes through your nose and travels down deep into your lungs. Your lungs continue to expand until they are content and just as the last inch is filled, you exhale and all the air, along with your problems and stress, rushes out as if it had somewhere else to be.

Other than being one of the main functions that keep you alive, breathing can help put you in a state of relaxation no matter what type of day you had. This is why so many swear by the effects of yoga and meditation, which have been around for thousands of years[98].

---

98 Salmon et al. 2009. "Yoga And Mindfulness: Clinical Aspects Of An Ancient Mind/Body Practice". Cognitive And Behavioral Practice

Both activities stress the importance of mindful breathing, which is the art of opening awareness to your breath, paying close attention to the air as you inhale in, and exhale out. Combined with yoga, mindful breathing has been observed to reduce stress, which helps to decrease risk for anxiety or depression, as well as help improve flexibility and muscle strength[99].

Still, there are people who are skeptical about its effectiveness as a practice. This is what led Dr. White from the Boston College School of Nursing to gather her team and get to the bottom of these effects.

She recruited 155 fourth and fifth grade girls and split them into two groups: an intervention group and a control group. Both groups met once a week for eight weeks, but only the intervention group practiced yoga and mindful breathing exercises.

At the end of the eight-week period, girls in the intervention group had reported higher self-esteem and coping skills than those in the control groups.[100]

Dr. Alessandro, a researcher at the University of Bologna, also noted the use of either of these activities to reduce stress in adults, while Dr. Khalsa, director of clinical studies at the

---

99 Ibid

100 White, Laura Santangelo. 2012. "Reducing Stress In School-Age
     Girls Through Mindful Yoga". Journal Of Pediatric Health Care 26

Laureate Institute for Brain Research, noted that yoga helped "reduce metabolic rate and lower oxygen consumption; also improving respiration and neuromuscular function."[101]

Although research is still being conducted, mindful breathing through yoga is a good way to get physical activity during your week, but what if you had trouble focusing on your breathing patterns because it was hard for you to breathe in general?

Due to the increased rise in obesity, this is a reality that is becoming more real, not just for people who want to practice this form of yoga, but to everyday people who feel doing everyday tasks now make breathing difficult.

French exercise physiologist, Mehdi Chlif, conducted a study to see the effects of obesity on breathing. He gathered thirty-two obese males and eighteen control subjects and ran tests measuring things such as breathing patterns and maximal inspiratory pressure, which tells us the strength of the diaphragm, the main muscle used by the lungs for breathing.

After examining the data, he found that maximal inspiratory pressure was significantly lower in obese individuals, and also noted that obesity can increase the need for oxygen for

---

101 "Principles And Practice Of Stress Management, Third Edition". 2019. Google Books

the respiratory muscles itself, meaning the energy cost of breathing was higher in these subjects than the control.[102]

People who are obese, and even those who are skinny and don't get enough aerobic exercise, may also suffer from something called dyspnea, or shortness of breath. People who struggle with this can experience chest tightening, difficult breathing, hyperventilation, and other uncomfortable side effects that can generally be seen after short bursts of physical activity.[103]

This can be a serious condition, as it is a precursor for many more threatening respiratory diseases such as bronchitis, severe asthma, or pneumonia, but worst of all it leaves you unable to do your favorite hobbies and activities for daily living.

Imagine trying to walk across your house to go to the bathroom and needing to stop to take a break because you were out of breath. That is the harsh reality for too many people around the country and one that could be mitigated by making sure your respiratory system is functioning properly by not smoking and doing your weekly aerobic exercise.

---

102 Chlif et al. 2009. "Effects Of Obesity On Breathing Pattern, Ventilatory Neural Drive And Mechanics". Respiratory Physiology & Neurobiology
103 "Trouble Breathing". 2019. Mayo Clinic.

Other than being the mechanism that powers our breathing, the lungs and respiratory system do much more. As you take a deep breath, your lungs fill with air, which carries about 21 percent of oxygen. The oxygen we breathe in is essential for metabolic activity, playing a pivotal role in the energy production process.

First, oxygen will diffuse into the bloodstream where red blood cells will transport them through the whole body whether that be to the muscles or other organs. The oxygen is then used as a vessel and combined with protons and carbon atoms, generally toward the end of the energy-making process, and is diffused back into the blood and heads back to the lungs to be exhaled as a waste product.[104]

The lungs are made up of many parts, but the smallest units in them are the tiny alveoli sacs. These sacs are surrounded by capillaries, the smallest type of blood vessel in the body, and it is at this point where all the diffusion between the circulatory and respiratory system occurs.[105]

It is amazing to see how both these body systems work together so seamlessly. Both have to work every day without any breaks

104 Pittman, Roland. 2011. "The Circulatory System And Oxygen Transport". Morgan & Claypool Life Sciences.
105 "How The Lungs Work | National Heart, Lung, And Blood Institute (NHLBI)". 2019. Nhlbi.Nih.Gov.

from the time you are born until the time you die, and what's crazier is that we have essentially no control over any of it.

Although these systems are paired so perfectly, they are still delicate. Without the proper maintenance, there is a real threat for major health problems.chronic obstructive pulmonary disease, or COPD, is a group of diseases that block airflow through the airways of the lungs. Individuals with these diseases generally suffer from shortness of breath, fatigue, wheezing, and coughing, and an increased chance of acquiring respiratory infections. What's worse is that these effects are generally agreed to be irreversible depending on the specificity of your condition, meaning there is no cure.[106]

Living with COPD can drastically decrease your quality of life, just ask anyone with emphysema. This type of COPD is caused by the destruction of your alveoli that we previously learned about. This makes diffusion into the bloodstream much harder and can make everyday life much more difficult. Normally, the alveoli have a lot of surface area due to how they are folded up. The folds create little pockets so more diffusion can occur, but when an individual suffers from emphysema the pockets are destroyed, greatly reducing the amount of oxygen that can be taken up at one time.[107]

---

106 "COPD | National Heart, Lung, And Blood Institute (NHLBI)". 2019. Nhlbi.Nih.Gov.
107 "Emphysema - Symptoms And Causes". 2019. Mayo Clinic

While the severity of this condition can vary, oftentimes, patients need more than just medications to help them get through their day, as some even need doses of oxygen supplementation through air tanks. Eventually, the condition can progress and if that is the case, then most will have to carry around an oxygen tank all the time. This heavy tank cripples your ability to move freely, ruining your quality of life and making you a prisoner of your disease.

Now this isn't meant to scare you, but instead to open all of our eyes just a little bit. With no known cure, we should be doing everything we can to prevent ourselves from getting diseases like COPD which are in part preventable. In fact, new research suggests that exercise might be the answer, even for those who have already acquired the disease, to help mitigate its effects.

Exercise rehabilitation is an effective way to help regain functionality after an injury and studies since the 1950s have noted its usefulness in pulmonary rehabilitation to help mitigate the effects of different lung conditions, but still many in the medical community remained skeptical.[108]

Recent articles provide an insight on the significance of physical activity on respiratory health. Of these, one meta-analysis of

108 Rochester et al. 2014. "Pulmonary Rehabilitation For Respiratory Disorders Other Than Chronic Obstructive Pulmonary Disease". Clinics In Chest Medicine

multiple research studies from 1950 to 2016 run by the Center of Expertise for Chronic Organ Failure in New Zealand found that "exercise training is the cornerstone of a comprehensive pulmonary rehabilitation program in patients with COPD." They continue to say that exercise is one of the most critical components to maintaining a patient's quality of life after being diagnosed with this condition, and explain that, "exercise training has been identified as the best available means of improving muscle function and exercise tolerance in patients with COPD."[109]

By being physical, you can still maintain a fulfilling and independent life. More shockingly is that exercise can also be the thing that saves your life. A recent study done by the pulmonary research institute in Germany recruited a cohort of 170 patients with stable COPD. They performed physical examinations on all of the patients and tested things such as lung function, physical activity level, and muscle and body composition, along with others to predict all-cause mortality percentages, or likelihood of death in the patients. They found that those who were more physically active and, therefore, more fit had a greater four-year survival rate, meaning they had less of a chance to die due to their condition.

What's even more amazing is that the researchers concluded that, "physical activity is the strongest predictor of all-cause

---

109 Spruit et al. 2016. "COPD And Exercise: Does It Make A Difference?". Breathe 12 (2): e38-e49. European Respiratory Society (ERS).

mortality in patients with COPD." These findings suggest that the single most important thing you can do to extend your life when living with COPD is exercise.

What we do have control over is the risk factors that can disrupt the harmony between these two systems. Certain behaviors can put you at a greater risk for heart disease and respiratory diseases such as smoking, eating food high in cholesterol and fat, and of course being physically inactive. Other conditions such as hypertension, type II diabetes, and some cancers can also be a result of these lifestyle choices. New studies also confirm that having low cardiorespiratory fitness is also a contributor to increasing your risk.

Due to the partnership that the cardiovascular and respiratory systems have, the likelihood of acquiring pathologies that are related to either of these systems increase when the other is damaged.

Some scientists point to the facts that diseases like COPD and other cardiovascular diseases (CVD) have many of the same risk factors such as smoking and having a poor diet, but other researchers think they have found clear correlation between the two conditions.

Scientists from the Division of Epidemiology and Public Health in the UK ran a study involving over 1.2 million people to find out if there was really any association between these conditions.

Through the use of primary care data, they gathered information on as many patients with COPD as possible. From there, they examined the percentage of people with CVD as well, and looked into how lifestyle choices such as smoking and diet could affect the results.

After comparing over one million people's data with the average risk factors for certain cardiovascular diseases, they found that, "individuals with COPD are substantially more likely to have pre-existing CVD, diabetes or a previous stroke and are at high risk," for other vascular diseases.[110]

With all these potential health risks, it is important that we do everything within our means to lower our chances of running into any trouble with our heart or lungs. This means saying no to cigarettes, eating healthy, and of course exercising regularly. Unfortunately, there is no other way to increase your cardiorespiratory health other than by exercising. The good news is that being active doesn't have to be as long and boring as most people make it out to be. The best way to make physical activity a habit is by trying to find something that

---

110 Feary JR, et al. 2019. "Prevalence Of Major Comorbidities In Subjects With COPD And Incidence Of Myocardial Infarction And Stroke: A Comprehensive Analysis Using Data From... - Pubmed - NCBI"

you enjoy doing. Although necessary for your body, it doesn't mean exercise can't be fun.

In fact, as long as you're not sitting, you will receive some benefit against fighting CVD. An article published by the Journal of the American College of Cardiology says, "Standing greater than 2 hours a day is associated with a 10% reduction of all-cause mortality," and, "decreases our risk of CVD by 32%."[111] Although not as effective as other types of physical activity, even just standing around can help save your cardiorespiratory system from potential harm by helping with circulation and, consequently, oxygen and carbon dioxide diffusion.

The more you move, the more benefits you'll receive, it's that simple, and it's not just benefits to help reduce CVD and COPD. The more you exercise, the more you work the muscles of the heart and lung as well. The heart being a muscle itself needs to be strong enough to contract and pump blood through the body, and the muscles surrounding the lungs are necessary to control breathing during respiration.

If these muscles are weak, then our ability to pump blood through our body and the amount of air we can take in will be impaired. Coupled with bad habits, such as smoking

---

111 Stamatakis et al. 2011. "Screen-Based Entertainment Time, All-Cause Mortality, And Cardiovascular Events". Journal Of The American College Of Cardiology

or long-term exposure to contaminants, it increases your chances for the conditions previously mentioned, and also so many more pertaining to both systems.

It's the little things that we often take for granted like being able to go down the steps of your home comfortably in the morning or being able to play catch with your sons or daughters. These freedoms are all attainable just by squeezing little bits of physical activity in whenever you can.

Do things like park on the opposite ends of the parking lot or have five minutes in your break planned out to take a walk or to dance to your favorite song. These small spurts can add up to a lot and meeting the recommended 150 minutes a week of activity will feel like a walk in the park, literally!

PART 2

MENTAL HEALTH

CHAPTER 6

BRAIN VERSUS COMPUTER

___

The brain is one of the most complex collection of circuits found on the planet and it allows us to harness the power equivalent to that of a super computer everywhere we go. By comparing the brain to the average computer, we begin to gain a sense of appreciation for just how complex of organisms we truly are.

A computer can have anywhere up to about 10 billion transistors. A transistor in basic terms is essentially one of the basic units needed for a computer.

The brain has around 100 billion neurons and 100 trillion synapses, or points of connections between neurons.[112]

While a computer mainly works in a serial fashion, the brain processes information both in a serial and parallel manner, meaning more parts of the brain can communicate and provide you with the best subsequent motor program for the task you need to perform. The brain's power and complexity are a scientific marvel on their own, but like all computers, sometimes there are problems that can arise from overuse, trauma, age, or just a random stroke of bad luck.

Now, when most people notice a problem with their computer, they don't waste a second thought and they head over to places such as the Apple Store or Best Buy. Some people even search YouTube for do it yourself solutions to figure out how to get their computers back up and running. No matter the situation, assuming the means are provided, everyone would fix their computer or phone at some point.

So, if that is the case, then why don't we invest more time into maintaining the most valuable "computer" that we own: our brains?

---

112 " Brain Vs. Computer ". 2019. Faculty.Washington.Edu.

One reason could be because today's society has a terrible addiction to the internet and their phones, especially the youth. It is estimated that 78 percent of American teens check their phone hourly and that 50 percent of teens believe they are addicted to their phones.[113]

This addiction can have real consequences on our brains if we are not careful. A study done by the University of Illinois also noted the negative health effects this can have on people. Researchers surveyed 300 college students and found that, "people who self-described as having really addictive-style behaviors toward the Internet and cellphones scored much higher on depression and anxiety scales."[114]

Researchers at the institute of psychological sciences also observed that people who reported higher internet dependency were also more likely to have depressive symptoms.[115] Depression can be a traumatic experience and it shouldn't take something as terrible as that for us to make a change.

However, the internet is not a completely terrible thing. It allows us to communicate across the world in seconds, store

---

113 "New Report Finds Teens Feel Addicted To Their Phones, Causing Tension At Home | Common Sense Media". 2019. Commonsensemedia.Org.

114 Banducci, Sarah. 2019. "News Bureau | ILLINOIS". News.Illinois.Edu.

115 Pantic, Igor. 2014. "Online Social Networking And Mental Health". Cyberpsychology, Behavior, And Social Networking

and look for information on virtually anything, and even allows us to buy and sell things without ever having to leave our house.

A study done by the Pew Research center observed that 79 percent of Americans now shop online or on their phones, which is up from 22 percent in the year 2000.[116] Even Amazon and Whole Foods have also recently teamed up and now you can buy your groceries online and have them delivered to your house.

Just like with so many other life conveniences, the internet, and specifically online shopping in this case, can also be abused. The more people are shopping online, the less they are walking in actual stores.

Many older adults get their weekly physical activity totals just from doing these types of errands. By removing that aspect of their lives, many would not meet weekly activity guidelines and, therefore, be putting themselves at a greater risk for various diseases.

It isn't just for online shopping, it almost feels like a necessity to be connected to the internet during the course of a

---

116 "Online Shopping And E-Commerce". 2016. Pew Research Center: Internet, Science & Tech.

day. During natural disasters and large power outages, many people feel lost whenever they are forced to be disconnected.

If you don't believe that society has a problem, then the next time you go out with your family or a big group ask everyone to put their phones in a bag and not touch them for the rest of the evening.

As soon as the idea is suggested, there is generally a look on the majority of people's faces. They seem almost irritated by the suggestion itself and some may even roll their eyes at you, wondering what point you are trying to make. Still, a good amount of people will come up with an excuse or say that they'll "put it on silent" or "keep it in their pocket."

Now, if this is you, there is nothing to be ashamed of because the majority of Americans, especially young adults, have been shown to have an increased dependency on their internet accessible device, but it is important to know the implications of what this type of addiction means.

The mental health aspect of these issues is still being learned, but we do know that there is a correlation between depression and those who are addicted to their phones, especially in cases where they are addicted to social media.[117]

117 Pantic, Igor. 2014. "Online Social Networking And Mental Health". Cyberpsychology, Behavior, And Social Networking

Many follow models and fitness gurus on social media, worshipping their bodies, and hoping to be like them one day. Oftentimes, however, these pictures have been altered in some way, whether through photoshop or elaborate filters. They post pictures of a body that is not humanly possible to achieve in a healthy way, which can affect the self-esteem of the youth when they realize that they will never be able to look like what they see on Instagram or Snapchat.

A rise in bullying has also been observed with the increase in social media use. Bullying is a terrible experience to go through and now with the internet it is easier than ever to have it happen to you. It is estimated that 75 percent of teens use Facebook and of the group, 54 percent experience cyberbullying.[118]

Cyberbullying is also harder to stop, as comments can be anonymous and there is less incentive for someone else to stop it if they aren't present with the bully and the victim in real life. Roughly 95 percent of teens have reported seeing some type of bullying, but not doing anything to stop it.[119]

This is even worse for kids who are overweight, as it is reported that 61 percent of overweight teens are bullied.[120]

---

118 "Teen Cyberbullying And Social Media Use On The Rise [INFO-GRAPHIC] - Rawhide". 2018. Rawhide.

119 "11 Facts About Cyberbullying". 2019. Dosomething.Org.

120 "Cyberbullying Awareness And Prevention ". 2019. Eluna Network.

Bullying can also lead to mental health problems in the future such as depression, low self-esteem, and eventually some even become suicidal.

It would be too difficult to try to ban social media use, after all, millions of people use these sites and they do help connect us like never before. Instead, we should enforce stricter anti-bullying regulations online and in schools and teach kids that words can end up ruining a person's life.

Another thing that may improve the mental health of these kids, and just people in general, is to become more physically active. Exercise can help decrease depressive symptoms and anxiety, raise your self-esteem, reduce your risk for dementia, and help with cognitive functions.[121]

For those who are bullied, joining a sports team can be a great way to make friends and also help with their social development. Sports allow us to create bonds and make new friends which will help decrease the likelihood for a variety of mental illness.

Through physical activity and team sports, we can help mitigate the effects of internet addiction and the negative aspects of social media. We need to understand that these

---

121 "Physical Activity Guidelines for Americans 2nd Edition". Health.Gov.

new advancements have an effect on our bodies and, more importantly, our brains. With the rise in awareness for mental health, we need to understand that we should care for our brains like our life depends on it, because in reality it does.

CHAPTER 7

FOCUS IN ON A BETTER MOOD

———

"No matter what people tell you, words and ideas can change the world."

—ROBIN WILLIAMS

Adored by many, Robin Williams was one of the most iconic actors of this past generation. He starred in films like *Dead Poet's Society*, *Good Will Hunting*, and too many others to list. He often inspired us with his words on and off the screen reminding people all over the world to, "seize the day," and to conquer our dreams.

To everyone's dismay, Williams committed suicide on August 11, 2014.[122]

As someone who grew up watching his movies, it didn't make any sense to me. Anytime you saw him on the screen he was happy, making someone laugh, or motivating others to be their best self, so how could this be? As I was reading an article shortly after his death, I came across a quote by Williams reading:

"I think the saddest people always try their hardest to make people happy. Because they know what it's like to feel absolutely worthless and they don't want anybody else to feel like that."

It began to make more sense, as those mental illnesses don't discriminate no matter our sex, religion, or the color of our skin. It was also later revealed that Williams suffered from Lewy body dementia at the time of his death. This disease causes protein deposits to build up in nerve cells, which in turn cause deterioration in memory, thinking, and movement. Combined with his depression and other facts, Williams was driven to do something that nobody wanted.[123]

---

122 "Robin Williams | American Comedian And Actor". 2019. Encyclopedia Britannica.
123 Williams, Susan Schneider. 2016. "The Terrorist Inside My Husband's Brain". Neurology 87

Other types of dementia, such as Alzheimer's and Parkinson's, all attack the brain cognition and function. In later stages, these diseases can even cause hallucinations, inability to talk or swallow, and even forgetting who family members are entirely.[124] The news only gets worse as these diseases are only becoming more common. Alzheimer's is the sixth leading cause of death in the US as of 2018, and has affected many families, including my own grandpa. Currently, there is no cure for these conditions, but research has been increased and some potential ways to slow down the effects of these diseases have been found, one of the more successful ones being exercise.

One study published in the *Journal of the American Medical Association (JAMA)* aimed to dig deeper into the effects of exercise on these forms of dementia. Head of the psychiatric department at the University of Melbourne, Dr. Nikola Lautenschlager, recruited 138 participants in an intent-to-treat analysis to see if an exercise intervention could mitigate the effects of these conditions. She prescribed a twenty-four-week home exercise program for individuals with the disease and compared it to those in a usual care group by testing their memory through a series of tests.

She found that the group that participated in the exercise intervention had scored much higher on their memory and

---

124 "Types Of Dementia". 2019. Alzheimer's Disease And Dementia

cognitive tests than those in the usual care group.[125] Other analysis published in the *Journal in Clinical Neurology* reviewed many different clinical tests and found that physical activity delays the onset of Alzheimer's and dementia in older people, and even saw individual risk of developing AD decrease by 45 percent.[126]

Another big factor contributing to the rise in research for these neurodegenerative diseases have been the association with athletes who suffered concussions in their past and prevalence of chronic traumatic encephalopathy (CTE). CTE is caused by repeated injuries to the head and, like the other diseases mentioned, it can cause loss of mental cognition, depression, and suicidal thoughts.[127]

This has been an especially big concern for a lot of contact sports where blows to the head are common. Soccer, football, rugby, lacrosse, and many others are all contact sports that can put you in situations where head injuries are more likely. The media has really put the spotlight on the National Football League (NFL) to do more research to ensure the safety of its players, as more and more retired professional athletes, not

125 Lautenschlager et al. 2008. "Effect Of Physical Activity On Cognitive Function In Older Adults At Risk For Alzheimer Disease". JAMA

126 Paillard et al. 2015. "Protective Effects Of Physical Exercise In Alzheimer's Disease And Parkinson's Disease: A Narrative Review". Journal Of Clinical Neurology 11

127 What Is CTE?". 2015. Concussion Legacy Foundation

just from football, have complained about headaches, memory loss, depression, and many others even acquire dementia later on in life[128]. These symptoms have begun to scare away youth participations in football as more and more parents feel like the possible risk that come along with these particular sports are becoming too high to involve their children. Some have even gone as far to declare this as a "national public health crisis."

As someone who had played football for ten years of my life, I thought I understood the risks that came along with signing up, but oftentimes parents and participants are not truly aware of the long-term effects of these risks. I definitely wasn't and it took me until I came to college to truly understand the implications of these repeated blows to my head. Regardless, I still haven't lost my love for football and I believe that it's anyone's right to play the sports they love as long as they, and their guardians, are knowledgeable of the repercussions.

So, if you are determined to play a sport with a likelihood for repeated head injuries, or if you have already played a sport that was susceptible to these types of traumas, what can you do now? Surely there has to be a way to provide some preventative measure against acquiring these side effects and

---

128 Ibid

diseases that we can all do. Thankfully, the answer is something that is free and accessible to anyone, anywhere, not surprisingly, it's also exercise.

Researchers have found out that the more you meet your recommended levels of physical activity and the more exercise you do in general, the bigger your prefrontal cortex and hippocampus get. The hippocampus plays a major role in memory formation and learning, while the prefrontal cortex is responsible for the personality traits that make you an individual. These areas of the brain that are benefited by physical activity are also the most susceptible areas for neurodegenerative diseases. By exercising and building a stronger hippocampus, you fight against the likelihood of deterioration and, therefore, memory loss and all the other terrible side effects that go with these types of diseases.[129]

During a TedX Talk in New Orleans, Wendy Suzuki, a neuroscientist from New York University described exercise, "as a supercharged 401K for your brain," continuing to joke that, "it's even better because it's free." The issue with humans is our innate need for instant gratification. We lack patience as a society and the advances in our technology are allowing us to receive information and services almost at an instant,

129 "The Aging Hippocampus: Interactions Between Exercise, Depression, And BDNF - Kirk I. Erickson, Destiny L. Miller, Kathryn A. Roecklein, 2012". 2019. The Neuroscientist.

which only help to reinforce that problem. She stresses, however, that making this "investment" in your brain will improve your quality of life as an older adult and decrease your risk for dementia, as well as many other diseases.[130]

Suzuki originally focused her research on memory function and had little interaction with how exercise affects human physiology, that was until one day she went white water rafting and noticed she was the weakest link of the group that she was rafting with. She was frustrated with this reality and when she got back ashore, she vowed to herself she would never be the weakest link ever again, finally giving her the motivation she needed to go to the gym. As she began her workouts, she noticed something strange that would happen after she began going to the gym. Her mood was boosted and her attention was better after she returned from her workout. At first, she thought it may be a fluke, but after consistently having these feelings post-workout, she then shifted her research focus on how exercise affects the brain, so that way she could find out what was really going on.

So, she began gathering as much data and running experiments to see the change in brain function after a workout. She first observed how neurotransmitters were influenced immediately after a workout. Neurotransmitters are just a

---

130 "The Brain-Changing Benefits Of Exercise | Wendy Suzuki". 2019

fancy way of saying the chemical messengers in your brain, so she was essentially seeing how our brains would communicate between itself and the rest of your body after a workout. Her research team found an increase in dopamine, which is responsible for many things, but is often associated with that "feel good" feeling we have after a reward. Dopamine is not the only neurotransmitter that we see released after a workout, as others include serotonin, which is good for sleep regulation, and norepinephrine, which helps to regulate blood sugar and body composition, just to name a few.[131]

Exercise also combats the effect of when there is too much of a certain neurotransmitter in the brain. Excessive cortisol can cause corrosive damage to your brain and is infamously known for being caused by too much stress. If these levels are consistently above the standard, it can lead to higher risks of depression and dementia. Every time you're physically active you decrease net levels of cortisol in the brain. This overall decrease in cortisol helps to fight against our risk for these conditions and slow the occurrence of them, and even hopefully keeping them from ever happening.[132]

The body goes through a similar change when you eat something high in sugar, such as candy or ice cream, and if you

---

131 Ibid
132 "2.11 Exercise: Nature's Medicine For Depression And Stress".
     2019. Youtube.

think about it, that makes a lot of sense. Nothing can soothe a person's soul better than their favorite dessert after a stressful day. Your stomach is overjoyed as you take that first bite, and an avalanche of dopamine is released in your brain, almost telling you that everything will be fine, no matter how many times your coach, boss, or teacher yelled at you today. Exercise is great because it gives that feeling of joy, but instead of taking calories in, you're burning them instead.[133]

An increase in dopamine not only helps your mood, but also helps your focus and attention. Wendy Suzuki's research team ran experiments to show that your attention span can be boosted for up to two hours after a workout.[134] This can be a big advantage, especially in an age where test scores seem to be everything, and students seem to be resorting to anything including buying prescription medication such as Adderall just to get a leg up. Taking drugs that aren't prescribed specifically to you can be very dangerous, as it can upset fragile chemical balances in the brain. Instead of doing something to hurt yourself, why not go for a run or just walk around the block? This will not only help improve your focus, but improve your overall health as well.

This increase in dopamine can also be great with people with Attention Deficit Hyperactivity Disorder or ADHD which

---

133 Ibid
134 "The Brain-Changing Benefits Of Exercise | Wendy Suzuki". 2019

is a disease that is generally affected by irregular dopamine regulation in the body. People diagnosed with this condition generally have a difficult time focusing their attention on one thing for extended periods of time. By exercising, you naturally increase dopamine levels and, therefore, your focus will also increase without any potential side effects of taking medications that have been seen to influence a person's mood, eating habits, and sleep schedule.[135]

So, next time you can't seem to focus when your studying for a big exam or prepping for that meeting at work, remember that just by getting up and moving around for a little bit, you can help yourself save hours of unproductively staring at your work.

---

135 "Physical Activity Guidelines for Americans 2nd Edition". Health.Gov.

CHAPTER 8

SWEAT OUT YOUR
PROBLEMS

———

Depression can often be a complicated issue.

Since we began to study this disease, people have argued
over what drives people to be depressed. Some hypothesize
that it is a chemical imbalance in the brain that affects their
mood and outlook, while others point to it being caused
by some type of life event or stressor, such as work or a
traumatic experience. Some people even blame side effects
caused by certain medications to cause depressive episodes
to begin.

What we are finding more and more, however, is that depression is caused by a combination of these things, and it can

be more layered and complex than just having something like the common cold.

Regardless of the main cause, we can all agree that depression is not something to be taken lightly, as roughly 300 million people across the globe have some sort of depression.[136] Depression often works in tandem with another mental illness, such as anxiety, which affects 40 million adults in the US today. In fact, depression and anxiety are two of the most common mental illnesses of the common era, as they affect 6.7 percent and 18.1 percent of the population age eighteen and older, respectively.[137]

Both of these conditions can make someone's life torturous, as people who suffer from them can find themselves feeling sad all the time, have a loss of interest in things they used to love, and low self-esteem. Depression can also suppress your appetite, mess with your sleep patterns and focus, and in the worst cases lead to suicidal thoughts and death.[138]

Depression only affects those who have had an unsuccessful life is a stigma. Events such as failure in a relationship or job are viewed as the cause for someone to go down this dark path. This, however, could not be more far from the truth, as even

136 "Depression". 2018. Who.Int.
137 "Data on behavioral health in the United States" 2019. Apa.Org.
138 "Depression". 2019. Google Books.

those that appear to have it all when standing from the outside looking in, can be struggling with either of these conditions.

These social stigmas end up doing a lot of harm because they discourage people who are struggling with their mental health from opening up and seeking help. They fear that if they admit to having a hard time, people will cease to view them as successful, or as a role model.

For one man, the story of finding the courage to be open about his mental illness did not come easy. Growing up playing basketball, the culture of the game insisted that he pocketed his emotions and never talked about his feelings, especially when out on the court. This basketball player is none other than National Basketball Association (NBA) champion and all-star, Kevin Love.

"Be strong and be a man," people would always say to him. This caused him to suppress any feelings that told him he needed to seek help, bottling it up so many times that it became second nature at one point. He says, "These values about men and toughness are so ordinary that they're every-where…and invisible at the same time, surrounding us like air or water. They're a lot like depression or anxiety in that way." Never getting the help he so desperately needed, he locked up his personal problems, only causing his issues to become worse leading to his anxiety and depression to only continue to get the best of him. It wasn't until he finally opened up did he begin to see improvement in his life saying, it was "the most important thing" he did.[139]

His battle was daily, but the catalyst to changing his mind about becoming more vocal about his conditions came on November 5th during a game against the Hawks on national television, when he suffered a panic attack mid game. He knew, "something was off right after tip off," and headed to the locker room early, never returning to the game. When asked to recall the event, he says, "I felt like everything was spinning like, my brain was trying to climb out of my head. The air felt thick and heavy. My mouth was like chalk." He was rushed to the hospital where all tests came back negative, but he knew he wasn't fine.

He had struggled with mental illness as a kid, but never really knew it, or understood what it meant. He recalls that, "he would be gone for a few weeks," in his room not talking or interacting with anyone. Combined with growing up with stigmas and the pressure to be an all-star, Love's condition was silently building up until finally erupting out of control during that game against the Atlanta Hawks.

As the dust settled, Kevin struggled with what to do next, but said it was important that he "pass the mirror test," as he

139 "Kevin Love Opens Up In Exclusive Interview About Mental Health Issues In The NBA [FULL] | ESPN". 2019. Youtube.

called it, for him to be happy. He wanted to look into the mirror and be content with his true self. He was tired of putting on a façade and displaying a different face to the world. Love said that, "only by admitting who we are do we get what we really want," and it was during this realization that he knew that he needed to share his story. Kevin followed his heart and wrote a piece for the *Players Tribune* called, "Everyone is going through something," followed by doing a one-hour ESPN special which I encourage you to read and watch. It is a short letter detailing his struggles with his mental illness and how he has navigated his life with depression and anxiety. He stresses the need for a strong support system and to not be afraid of the stigma surrounding mental illness, as he not only says that it can make you a better basketball player, but it gives you the "freedom" to live a healthy life.[140]

Kevin Love is not the only high-profile athlete to share how he feels about mental illness, as others like San Antonio all-star Demar Derozan, and twenty-eight-time Olympic medalist Michael Phelps have accomplished similar acts of bravery. Both also highlight their struggles with depression and anxiety reaching a point where Phelps even says, "I didn't have self-love, I didn't have self-confidence, and I didn't like who I saw in the mirror...It got to a point where I didn't want to be alive," but instead of giving up he knew he "needed to make a

---

140 "Everyone Is Going Through Something | By Kevin Love". 2019. The Players' Tribune

change," just like Kevin Love and many of the unrecognized heroes that came before him.[141]

What's also been so fascinating to see is that people like Phelps and Love, although being an Olympic hero and NBA champion respectively, still suffer through the same conditions as every other human in the world. To many, having fame, money, and everything that comes with being a super athlete should mean that it would be seemingly impossible to suffer from depression. The athletes often put on a mask for the public, but it is important to note that they are just as human as any of us are.

In many ways I think that is what they were trying to accomplish by stepping out of their comfort zone and speaking on this topic. They want to make a point to say that these mental illnesses do not have a target demographic in mind. Its ruthless and energy-sucking abilities will attack anyone who lets it, but hopefully by using the power of exercise and the strategies that famous athletes like Phelps and Love discussed, we can help to prevent depression from getting the chance to ruin our days.

So what if like these individuals you suffer from depression or anxiety too? Today, the solution is usually some type of

141 "Michael Phelps Opens Up About Struggle With Depression | TODAY". 2019. Youtube

medication prescribed by a psychiatrist or medical professional. Some even chose to pay for professional counseling through the use of some type of therapy, but these methods often prove to be very costly. Medication can also be expensive, depending on your insurance plan, sometimes making going to the doctor even more trouble than it is worth.

The cost is not the only concern, as there are often side effects that come alongside the use of various medications. Many of us have seen those commercials for medications at one point or another in our lives, and if you've been "fortunate" enough to have seen one, then you'll never forget the whispering voice that sneaks in and tells you all the harmful side effects of the drug at the end of the commercial. It's as if just because the side effects are being murmured while the person enjoys a blissful walk in the park, over an aesthetic background makes the side effects any less harmful or real. So, when the common side effects include your symptoms worsening and even death, why do we continue to allow ourselves to take the risk?

What's even worse is that a lot of common medications have often underperformed in clinical tests when compared to placebos. Multiple meta-analyses, which is just an examination of multiple sets of data from different independent studies, have found that some antidepressants do not work as well as previously reported and the difference between the placebo and the drug are not as wide as we once believed.[142] Although the Food and Drug Administration (FDA) provides evidence of data that supports a larger gap between efficacy in placebos versus antidepressants on their website, a non-industry study found the effectiveness of placebos in certain trials to be much higher, one meta-analysis run by Cambridge university and university college London's Dr. Joanna Moncrieff wrote that, "they are barely superior to placebo in randomized trials, and differences are unlikely to be clinically relevant."[143]

Dr. Arif Khan from the Duke University psychiatry department also examined multiple studies comparing effects of placebos to medications and found that at best, "effect size of current antidepressant trials that include patients with major depressive episode" to be "approximately 0.30." That means only 30 percent of people find that these medications truly work to make their depression better.[144]

Some researchers even question the physiological validity of the effect of these medications saying, "there is no

142 Wegner M, et al. 2019. "Effects Of Exercise On Anxiety And Depression Disorders: Review Of Meta- Analyses And Neurobiological Mechanisms. - Pubmed - NCBI
143 Timim et al. 2018. "Network Meta-Analysis Of Antidepressants". The Lancet 392
144 Khan, Arif, and Walter A. Brown. 2015. "Antidepressants Versus Placebo In Major Depression: An Overview". World Psychiatry 14

current evidence that any sort of drug specifically targets an underlying biological abnormality, and whether there is an underlying brain state or states specific to the experience of depression." Essentially, from analyzing the data, Dr. Moncrieff believes that we are going about the treatment of depression and anxiety the wrong way.[145] This is not to discredit the significant help prescription medications can have on patients, but what he alludes to in the quote and further explained in his analysis is that we continue to treat the symptoms of the ailment, but not the cause of them.

Now, these concepts are still argued over, and in every study you find that is published by an accredited scientific journal it says that there, "is still a need of evidence based research in the field," or that, "a long term study is needed to assess the true benefits of the drug." These are just ways to make sure we all know that they may have found a correlation, but not necessarily causation to the onset of depression.

Causation means that one particular event directly caused another to happen, while correlation means these two events influence each other, but generally indirectly or with other variables playing a role. Many different body system

---

145 Moncrieff, Joanna. 2018. "Against The Stream: Antidepressants Are Not Antidepressants – An Alternative Approach To Drug Action And Implications For The Use Of Antidepressants". Bjpsych Bulletin 42

reactions can be influencing chemical changes in the body at once, so it is difficult to get the whole picture drawn out and understood. It's most common in scientific research to find a correlation between two variables, but it is much more difficult to prove causation, especially when you first begin a new set of trials and experiments.

The same is true for our bodies, as it's hard to pinpoint the sole causation of a problem when you're sick. The body is a complex interaction of millions of subunits and like a mosaic, everything works in tandem to give you the bigger picture. No one piece of your body can stand alone and when one system is affected by something it will then indirectly effect many of the systems adjacent to it. The body, although able to accomplish unbelievable acts of strength, can also be very fragile, as there is a delicate balance that must be maintained.

This is largely the reason why it makes it especially difficult to treat mental disorders in the first place. First and foremost, we are only scratching the surface of the understanding of how the underlying mechanisms of our brain work and without knowing what's really going on we can't synthesize effective solutions. The other difficulty is making medicines that only directly affect the part of the body that is malfunctioning.

As we mentioned earlier, the body systems are constantly interacting and there are millions of subunits communicating with each other at one time. By effecting something like transmission of a certain neurotransmitters you are not only affecting that specific receptor in regards to depression, but also everywhere else in the body. The receptors also communicate with other parts of the body as well, so by blocking its transmission you can also be cutting off other essential communication pathways for body regulation and homeostasis.[146]

Of course, the body generally has "back-up plans" in case things go wrong, but it is important to at least acknowledge its effects on the body, no matter how small. A chain is only as strong as its weakest link and we should remember that saying as we make important decisions regarding our health, no matter what it might be.

So, now we have a level of understanding for how complex and delicate the human body really is. We also know that these drugs carry potentially harmful effects and their effectiveness has been shown to vary through different studies.

Still there is way to reducing your chance of ever getting depression or anxiety, or at least mitigating their effects. Physical activity is, not surprisingly, that mechanism that can help millions of people around the world take back control over their lives.

---

146 "The Nervous And Endocrine Systems Review". 2019. Khan Academy

Exercise is the only way to not only take an individual and improve their symptoms of depression and anxiety, but even help benefit their body in other ways at the same time. The Centers for Disease Control (CDC) says that those who participate in their 150 minutes of moderate weekly exercise are at a lower risk for depression and have shorter stints of depressive symptoms.[147] Being physically active can also help to improve state anxiety, which is anxiety you feel in a certain situation, and trait anxiety, which is frequent anxiety that stays with you and attacks randomly.

To make sure this was the case, many researchers have tried to perform different studies to see what the effect of exercise is on anxiety and depression. In a meta-analysis run by European sports scientist, Mirko Wegner, examined studies from over 42,000 people with anxiety and over 48,000 thousand people with depression. He found that there is evidence to support the use of exercise for treatment in both conditions, and especially in depression. He calculated that after accounting for all the studies, the effect size for exercise in this study was 0.56, meaning that 56 percent of people received some benefit to their depressive symptoms.[148]

147 "Physical Activity Guidelines for Americans 2nd Edition"
148 Wegner M, et al. 2019. "Effects Of Exercise On Anxiety And Depression Disorders: Review Of Meta- Analyses And Neurobiological Mechanisms. - Pubmed - NCBI

When comparing the effect of antidepressants on depression with the meta-analysis from earlier, we see that exercise was actually a more effective method in reducing depressive symptoms.

Stress is one of the contributors to depression and other serious pathologies, and whether it be problems at work, school, or at home the stressors of life never seem to take a break. Under stress, the body releases a hormone called cortisol. Cortisol, in appropriate doses, helps regulate homeostatic functions in the body, but in excess can be detrimental to our mental health. [149]

Prolonged increased cortisol levels have been associated with promoting dementia and depression in patients. A study that was published by the *Journal of Affective Disorders* was also done showing the effect of elevated cortisol level in patients with major depressive disorder (MDD), and its effect on memory. The study found that patients with depression were observed to have a greater amount of basal level cortisol than participants with no diagnosis.[150]

An indirect relationship was also found between participants with high cortisol levels and their hippocampal volume. The

149 "Chronic Stress Puts Your Health At Risk". 2019. Mayo Clinic.
150 Harris et al. 2006. "Physical Activity, Exercise Coping, And Depression In A 10-Year Cohort Study Of Depressed Patients". Journal Of Affective Disorders 93

Hippocampus is located in the brain and is responsible for aspects of memory storage. With the relationship observed between these conditions, there were concerns that patients with depression would also suffer an increased risk of memory impairment compared to healthy individuals.

The researchers continued to conduct the study and the results confirmed the original hypothesis and more. Those with MDD had a higher level of Cortisol Awakening Response (CAR) which elevates cortisol levels in the brain.[151] As we learned previously, high cortisol levels lead to lower Hippocampal volumes, which ultimately means decreased memory function. What was even more astonishing was that the effect of stress on these conditions was not only seen in patients with depression, but nondepressed subjects as well, meaning stress that causes elevated levels of cortisol can negatively impact healthy populations.

Many recent studies have observed the effect of exercise on hippocampal volumes and, not surprisingly, many of them note the benefits that exercise can have on your hippocampus. As you grow older, your hippocampus slowly begins to decrease in volume. This rate can be accelerated like we alluded to before, with influence from things like stress, but until recently we didn't have any method to slow down its deterioration.

---

151 Dedovic et al. 2015. "The Cortisol Awakening Response And Major Depression: Examining The Evidence". Neuropsychiatric Disease And Treatment, 1181

Recently, experimental results have shown how exercise can play a major role in slowing down the decrease in hippocampal volumes. An examination of fourteen major studies, in which 737 subjects were examined, provided evidence that exercise helps fight against hippocampal decay, especially on the left side, when compared to control conditions.[152] The implications of these studies shouldn't be underestimated, as this shows that exercise is essentially the only proven way to protect the longevity of your memory and protect against deadly neurodegenerative diseases.

Even with the positive effects, exercise can have on the mind, it is still not perfect. Oftentimes, people who get sufficient physical activity can suffer from mental conditions, just like in the case of Kevin Love and Michael Phelps. In their interviews, they mention that their respective sports came with too much pressure and work and ceased to be enjoyable. It wasn't that they didn't like the sport, but rather they didn't enjoy what came with it at such a high of a level.

This should be another lesson to us, as sports can be a medicine for our mental health, but only if it brings some enjoyment to your life. When participating in a sport, if it ever begins to cause more stress than pleasure, it may be time to

152 Erickson et al. 2011. "Exercise Training Increases Size Of Hippocampus And Improves Memory". Proceedings Of The National Academy Of Sciences 108

take a break or try something new. The key to receiving the full platoon of benefits and to make exercise a habit, is to find something you love to do, so that it doesn't feel like a job, but a hobby. Being physically active can change how our minds work on the inside if we do it correctly.

CHAPTER 9

SHIFTING FOCUS FROM FATNESS TO FITNESS

———

One of the most important reasons to learn about all the advantages that being physically active has to offer is because knowledge is an essential part in helping you to change perspectives, and see things in a new light.

Building this knowledge is not only good for changing the negative feelings toward exercise into positive ones, but it also helps change why you think doing exercise is important in the first place. In today's society, it is hard to have our priorities set solely on our health when it comes to physical activity. This is partially because we are flooded with information from all sorts of outlets such as social media, radio, and TV stations that try to influence our thinking.

For example, no matter what you're watching or hearing, there are generally commercials that play periodically, whether it be for various clothing brands, car companies, or whatever. These companies use marketing tactics through advertisements that generally display stereotypical "good looking" people using or wearing their product. These people are often in shape and look as if they are living in luxury or happiness just because they are using that company's product. They hope to convey the feeling that, you too can feel rich and beautiful by following what the models do on TV, and by doing so they send a kind of subliminal message that dictates what society deems as beautiful. This can be dangerous as often times these new standards can oftentimes create unrealistic expectations that we feel we must meet.

In the youth, this is especially troubling, considering the fact that kids are malleable and more susceptible to being influenced by the media, friends, and adults. So, you can see that there is a problem with consistently showing children pictures of photoshopped models on huge skyscraper-sized billboards. This creates feelings of inferiority not only just in children, but in the rest of society as well. It almost feels as if we worship them in a way, hoping to one day have the same body as them. The reality is that no one can look that skinny without resorting to unhealthy measures, and by drilling these images into the eyes of the public we can inadvertently be sending the wrong message.

Some say that "harmless" advertisements have an impact on the welfare of a child's mind and that we are overreacting in connecting these ideas. To those people who doubt the effects that this type of imagery can have, I point to a study done by the Professional Association of Child Care and Early Years (PACEY) that showed that, "children as young as three expressed dissatisfactions and concern with their appearance and their body."[153] Now I don't know about you, but I was not very intelligent as a three-year-old, and like most of us, I was still trying to figure out my left from my right. The idea that even a three-year-old can pick up on these societal cues from their environment and deem themselves as inferior to others is rather alarming, and it is something that should raise questions as to what we are doing and its implications to society as a whole.

No wonder kids grow up believing they need to be skinny. It's all that they have ever seen on TV since they were able to start making sense of what is going on in the world, skinny people were almost always the famous ones. It's not only due to TV, as we further reinforce these ideas by having routine checks at doctor's offices that ask questions about weight instead of fitness.

One of the most common measures taken at the doctor's office is a called a body mass index, or more commonly

153 Why Fitness Is More Important Than Weight | Leanne Spencer | Tedxwandsworth". 2019. Youtube.

referred to as BMI, which is just an equation that gives you a number based on your height and weight. Depending on the number that is calculated, you can either be classified as underweight, normal weight, overweight, or obese.[154]

These measurements can often give a misleading picture to what is really going on in the body and to what a person's fitness level actually is. Most people believe that to be healthy you need to be in the right BMI range or else you are still at risk for many conditions, but that is far from the truth. It is very common, especially for kids, to be considered very fit, but still have a BMI that is considered overweight or even bordering obese. In fact, the measure of BMI itself is a prehistoric way to judge someone's state of health, as it doesn't take into account age or percentage of muscle versus fat in your body.

This focus on achieving the perfect body and trying to get your "numbers" to display those that are considered healthy by a chart on a piece of paper is leading people to find unhealthy ways to achieve their dream bodies. Things like depriving your body of important nutrients either through cutting out food groups like carbs, or not eating in general, will lead to weight loss that is not sustainable, or even worse, lead to terrible eating disorders such as anorexia or bulimia, which can help foster depression as well.

---

154 "Defining Adult Overweight And Obesity | Overweight & Obesity | CDC". 2019. Cdc.Gov.

The pressure of needing to get to the perfect weight is also made worse by the social setup that's in place in schools and youth sports all around the country. About half of participants in a new study conducted by researchers at the Rudd Center for Food Policy and Obesity at the University of Connecticut identified weight as the most common reason youths are bullied by their peers.[155]

This can make you feel as if it is you versus the rest of the world, and even though it may just be one individual who isn't mature enough to see what his comments can do to a person, it still makes you feel like you are all alone. You begin to group exercise with those "skinny" or "normal" people who just don't understand what you may be going through and you begin to dislike them and yourself because of that. The negative attitude builds towards going to the gym or for a run because you'll have to see the people who torment you based on your features alone and as a result you end up never going.

The fact is that we are all influenced by the opinions of others to some degree, but by understanding the benefits of moving around, you can cement your commitment to going to the gym or doing whatever other type of activity that can provide you with the tools to add years on to your life.

---

155 "Here's The One Thing That Makes A Kid More Likely To Be Bullied In School". 2019. Takepart

This idea of bullying in schools is just one example of how our experiences can lead to our distaste with exercise. People generally don't like physical activity for a variety of reasons and negative experiences can manifest themselves in many different scenarios and environments. So, what if instead of thinking negatively of the physical activity, we rearrange our perception of what it could do for us?

That's exactly what Leanna Spencer, a personal trainer from England, decided to do. She describes her struggles with alcoholism as, "a very dark and difficult time in her life." Alcoholism is often an all-consuming disease that can take over a person's life, potentially causing them to lose their job, hurt relationships, and cause damage to their bodies. People with this disease are at higher risks for depression and other mental disorders and, like Leanna herself, become dependent on it until it becomes unhealthy. Fortunately, she was eventually treated for her condition in March of 2012 and she says that, "exercise became the very corner stone for my successful recovery. Instead of drinking bottles of wine every night I used exercise to change how I felt about myself." She continues, saying that exercise was a wonderful mechanism to build resilience and that it really helped her get through her tribulation.[156]

---

156 Why Fitness Is More Important Than Weight | Leanne Spencer | Tedxwandsworth". 2019. Youtube.

Through her fitness journey, she also experienced the effects of exercise on people who didn't seem to have the ideal body shape. She recalls going to an acrobatic performance seeing people, "perform the most incredible feats of athleticism, strength and bravery," and what stood out at the end of the show was not the amazing stunts she had just witnessed. Instead her focus was on the physiques of these performers as some were out right muscular, as you would expect, while "some had a layer of fat over their abdominals, and on their inner thighs," all very characteristic of "normal" nonathletic people. These average-looking individuals were able to do some of the most extraordinary things with their bodies and this thought caused something to click in Leanna's brain.

She realized at the moment that we had made a mistake. By worrying so much about things like our appearance, our BMI score, and the opinions of our peers, "we forgot about what's really important and that's the health of our bodies on the inside." She goes on to ask, "what if we focused our attention to what we can achieve with our bodies rather than what they look like, what if we moved the focus from fatness to fitness?"[157]

By shifting our attention to our fitness levels and what we can personally accomplish, we generate more positive thoughts and ideas. You begin to see results as you get stronger or

157 Ibid

faster, regardless of your body type. This feeling of success is rewarding and can build good habits that will not only stick with you, but also help allow you to reach and maintain a healthy weight.

This is not to dismiss the obesity epidemic seen across the world, especially in the United States. About two-thirds of Americans are either overweight or obese, which means that they are at a higher risk for pathologies including heart disease and diabetes.[158] While it is true that they are at a greater risk to get these conditions, it is not well understood whether the reason is due to obesity or if it is due to their sedentary lifestyle.

A study was conducted by the American Diabetes Association to try to further understand the mechanisms between obesity and our risk for death. They had a cohort of over 20,000 middle-aged men, and assessed their physical activity levels and followed up with them yearly. Over the course of eight years, they assessed each individual's risk for death and fitness level and the results were not as expected.

As you would expect, those who were fit and had a healthy BMI were at the lowest risk for all-cause mortality, but those who were obese and were still fit, actually had a lower chance of something going wrong than those who were

---

158 "Defining Adult Overweight And Obesity | Overweight & Obesity | CDC". 2019. Cdc.Gov.

more sedentary, but yet had a "healthy" BMI.[159] The results give insight on the power that being physically active has to offer us, as even those who are struggling with their weight can still help decrease their chance of death just by moving around!

A misconception about inactive people is that they are all obese. Although it is common for an inactive person to be overweight it is also very plausible for someone who is really skinny to be sedentary as well. This can be seen in cases with people who have bulimia, as they can be underweight individuals who use binging, and then purging to help prevent gaining weight. Sometimes these methods are used along with restricting one's diet, almost to the point of starvation just so they can keep the weight off.[160] Again, these conditions are made worse due to the beauty standards of our modern-day society. Many people with these conditions do not go to the gym either because they lack the energy and nutrients. They try to achieve their desired weight through these horrible techniques that end up hurting their bodies more and causing them to become more inactive.

Being inactive is especially important to consider in the older generations of adults. It is estimated that 31 million

159 Church et al. 2003. "Exercise Capacity And Body Composition As Predictors Of Mortality Among Men With Diabetes". Diabetes Care 27
160 "Bulimia Nervosa". 2017. National Eating Disorders Association.

Americans that are age fifty or older are inactive, which means they get no physical activity outside their activities for daily living.[161] Being inactive can be very harmful to the health of older adults and can cause muscle and bone deterioration to accelerate, as well as the likelihood of injury. Being sedentary also increases your likelihood of being disabled as researchers at Northwestern University say that, "for people 60 and older, each additional hour a day spent sitting increases the risk of becoming physically disabled by about 50 percent." In fact, so many people deal with disabilities now that, "every $1 in $4 spent on medical care is related to disability problems."[162]

This is truly alarming and is also a huge economic burden that can plague a family who is struggling to make ends meet. The sad part is that it can be prevented or at least slowed down just by consciously trying to sit less throughout the day. Millions of dollars could be saved, as well as improving the lives of millions, but for that to happen the focus must shift from fatness to fitness.

It's important that we change our mind-sets so we don't live and die by the number displayed on the scale. We know that no matter how overweight or underweight we get, what

161 "Adults Need More Physical Activity". 2019. Centers For Disease Control And Prevention
162 "NPR Choice Page". 2019. Npr.Org

truly matters is how we feel on the inside. You can still be unhealthy on the inside even if your BMI displays a "healthy" weight and at the end of the day making sure your body is functioning properly takes priority over having rock solid abs.

BMI along with many other measures should be used and viewed as a tool to give us a look into how we are doing, it should not be the end all be all of fitness tracking. Instead we should begin to measure how we feel on the inside and when we don't feel good we should try to get moving, as it is the only medicine that we can take to protect us against the fight against inactivity and all the nasty effects that it can have on our bodies.

CHAPTER 10

THE MIND'S EYE

Learning all about the benefits that physical activity can provide is great, but it is useless unless we can get people's mind-sets to change and incorporate that information. Many complain about the horrors of exercising and never really being able to find enjoyment in moving around. It seems that more and more people in today's world would rather break a sweat eating hot wings watching the game on the couch than actually going outside to shoot hoops or run around with their friends and family. Yet, there are still some people that still appreciate the early mornings, and wake up hours before work or school to go to the gym or run or do whatever that gets their heart rate up. This begs the question, what is it that makes these people different from one another?

The answer is still unknown, but one of the explanations scientists have formulated has to do with the lineage of the human race. For thousands of years, humans lived off the land as hunter-gatherers and large food surpluses were often hard to come by. With calories being scarce, the brain selected against unnecessary exercise, which could burn too much energy that people back in the day couldn't afford to lose. Scientists say that these evolutionary traits could have stuck with our DNA, making additional exercise always seem like a task, more than a hobby.[163]

Others hypothesis that it has to do with is how we perceive the world itself. Emily Balcetis, researcher and social psychologist at NYU, thinks it primarily may have to do with our vision and how that factors into what she calls your, "Mind's Eye." She gave a TED talk in New York in 2014 trying to explain just that as she starts by saying, "Vision is the most important and prioritized sense that we have. We are constantly looking at the world and we instantly know what is going on around us."[164]

To show us the importance of vision and how we all see things through our own "Mind's Eye" she presented an audience with a picture of a gentlemen during a Ted Talk she gave in New York in 2014. She asked the crowd what emotion

---

163 The modern obesity epidemic, ancestral hunter-gatherers, and the sensory/reward control of food intake."Psycnet. 2019.
164 "Why Some People Find Exercise Harder Than Others | Emily Balcetis". 2019. Youtube.

he was displaying on his face. A murmur went through the crowd as they discussed their opinions amongst each other, as they shared what they thought, coming up with a few different emotions. Let's try it out for ourselves, what do you see?

165

Her team had already surveyed 120 individuals before the presentation, asking them that exact question and like the crowd, the results were surprisingly mixed. No one could agree on the exact emotion the man in this picture was feeling. Most saw discomfort, but other common answers ranged from fearful and anxious to even feeling hopeful or

165 "Why Some People Find Exercise Harder Than Others | Emily Balcetis". 2019. Youtube.

empathetic. Her point was that perception was subjective, and what we think we see is actually filtered through our own mind's eye.

Our experiences and everyday interactions contribute to how our mind's eye thinks and this can alter our perceptions of the world. An example of how this works can be seen in another experiment run by Balcetis and her team. She surveyed hundreds of Americans right before the 2008 elections and asked them which pictures out of a set portrayed former President and then Candidate, Barack Obama, the closest. The pictures were the exact same with the only difference being whether Obama's skin was artificially lightened or darkened. She found that 75 percent of people who picked the artificially lightened picture voted for him during the election, while 89 percent of people who picked the pictures of Obama that were darker voted for McCain, the Republican Nominee.[166]

Now, this project was eye opening for many reasons. First, it showed that two people can look at a photo of the same exact person and physically see them as slightly different. The difference in their appearance is not because of any defect or difference in the anatomy of our eyes, but instead a difference in our life experiences that lead us to different

---

166 Ibid

subjective views of a person. The project also showed us that we are still a nation divided, where the color of our skin still seems to determine how we are judged in society. More specifically, not the color of our skin, but instead how people perceive the color of our skin and what it means to them, in their own minds eye. This problem is clearly so rooted in society that it is actually affecting our subconscious minds, and, therefore, mind's eye, to a point where we see the same person differently.

The political implications of Balcetis's project are enough to write a whole book about alone, but for our purposes, most importantly, this shows why some people hate to exercise and why some people can't live without it. The way the anatomy of the body is set up is that it only allows us to sharply see small areas of an image at any given time. Our vision can only focus in on an area as great as the surface of our thumb with our arm stretched out all the way. The rest of what we perceive the image to be, is actually our minds filling in the missing pieces. We use our past experiences and all the information stored in our neuronal tracts to fill in the gaps to what else is going on around us.[167] For this reason, perception of what we see is a subjective experience with everyone else filling in the gaps in the way their mind's eye tells them to. This could be one of the reasons that some people see

167 "Why Some People Find Exercise Harder Than Others | Emily Balcetis". 2019. Youtube.

something that reminds them of exercise and automatically feel demotivated, while others see some type of reminder and feel obligated to go to the gym as soon as possible.

Don't fear, as the mind's eye is impressionable due to the fact that it continues to learn from your experiences as you progress through life. That should give us comfort that hope is not lost, if you are part of the overwhelming majority that is reminded of exercise and automatically wants to shy away from it. Balcetis, once again, put her theories to the test by running another set of experiments where subjects had to estimate a distance to a finish line and then race to the point as fast as possible. In her first set of tests she compared fit individuals to those who reported being less active. The results showed that people who were in better shape actually saw the finish line as closer than their non-fit counterparts. It was amazing to see that just by getting into better shape, exercise not only became easier for your body, but for your mind too.

She decided to run the test again, but this time instead of only comparing their fitness levels, she also added another category; motivation. Again, participants estimated the distance they were standing from the finish line, and the results revealed something hopeful. Balcetis found that people who were motivated to participate in exercise saw the finish line as being closer, and those who were unmotivated, or had a negative outlook on being active consequently saw the finish line as being farther away.

This didn't just apply to fit individuals, as those who were categorized as unfit, but yet reported having motivation to be active, also saw the finish line as closer than those who were fit, but lacked motivation.[168]

Through her experiments, Balcetis helps us understand how human behavior can be influenced by mentality. Just by having a positive outlook we can make tasks that usually seem grueling much more manageable, and eventually even fun. Thinking positively not only makes exercise easier, but it alone can be very beneficial for your health.

Having a positive outlook was seen to decrease the likelihood of depression and stress, help immunity and cardiovascular health, and even increase your lifespan.[169] By pairing this mentality with exercise, you can double up on the good you're doing for your body and make life a little bit easier along the way.

---

168 Ibid
169 "How To Stop Negative Self-Talk". 2019. Mayo Clinic.

PART 3

SOCIAL HEALTH

CHAPTER 11

A SOCIAL INTRODUCTION

———

The influence of societal perspectives can actually change how we think and that is no different for how we view medicine. We see it only as a tool to cure physical illnesses, and only recently have people only considered medicine effective for mental illnesses. Still, humans often neglect the other aspect that is crucial for our well-being and health, our social lives. The Self-Determination Theory of psychology, which we talked a little bit about in previous chapters, also helps us conceptualize a human's innate psychological needs. These include autonomy (a sense of control), competence (or a feeling of worth), and relatedness (the need for social acceptance).[170] This theory

———

170 "Theory – Selfdeterminationtheory.Org". 2019. Selfdetermination-theory.Org

helps reinforce the importance of an individual's social life on their overall health and happiness.

Other models also stress the need for social acceptance as a basic human need, so if having a positive social experience is so essential the next question becomes, how can we achieve a healthy social life?

A good social life comes naturally for some individuals. These are people that grew up embracing the social scene rather than fearing it. These are the types of people who can strike up a conversation with complete strangers, and have no problem speaking in front of others. Being the center of attention is comfortable for them, but for others social interaction wasn't as easy; I know because I was one of those kids.

I always liked to describe myself as shy. Like so many, I never understood why socializing was so difficult for me. I always felt anxious and uneasy in social situations, especially when I was placed into a new setting. It always seemed like there was a war inside of my mind, battling for dominance over my personality. One side wanted to share all my comments and thoughts that crossed my mind while the other, fueled by my self-conscious, was too embarrassed or nervous to voice my opinion. Unfortunately, that side of me was the victor more often than not, and it forced me to bottle up my ideas and feelings, no matter what they may have been. The war in my head controlled me in every new situation I found myself in and a part of me felt like my freedom was being taken away.

Besides these negative feelings, keeping everything bundled up inside of you, can also be detrimental to your health. Previous studies have indicated that negative emotions can be linked to depression, anxiety, and recent studies by the Harvard School of Public Health and the University of Rochester have also found that suppressing these emotions can even increase your risk for heart disease and certain forms of cancer.[171] Everyone needs an outlet to relieve stress and oftentimes talking to someone is the best way.

Whenever I had a difficult day at work or school, where everything just seemed to not be going my way, I often found refuge when I talked to my brother. I would complain for hours about how my teacher never taught us anything on the tests, or how my boss had yelled at me for no reason.

As I got older, I realized two things; my boss generally had a good reason for yelling at me, but more importantly that my brother never said much during these conversations. Instead he would nod his head attentively and just let me get everything that I needed to off my chest, and it almost always made me feel better. Now, of course this is not to say that you can't

171 Srini Pillay, MD. 2016. "Managing Your Emotions Can Save Your Heart - Harvard Health Blog". Harvard Health Blog

relieve stress through other healthy outlets like music or art, but having a good social life can not only help you relieve that stress, but also take care of the human need of relatedness that we all long for to some degree.

So, why do some people have so much trouble in social settings? For many, it's a lack of self-confidence. This can be caused by many different things. Some aren't particularly happy with some aspect of themselves, which makes them fear judgment from other people. This could be due to their weight, sexuality, skill level, or whatever else they don't like about themselves.

For me, like many others across the world, being different was what made me self-conscious and fearful of social interactions. Growing up one of the few minorities in a community always made me feel like I was on the outside looking in. My parents were foreigners and our culture was significantly different than the lives of my classmates and although I was too young to understand what that meant, I still had this feeling lurking inside me letting me know I was different.

It wasn't until later on in my life that I started to embrace this difference as it was what made me unique, but early on, these feeling coupled with my naturally introverted personality always made it difficult making friends. I would often reflect on why I couldn't muster up the courage to go say hello to a new classmate or to the girl I had a crush, but yet I could never crack the code. It wasn't until much later in my life that I realized that it wasn't that I had a problem, but instead I just had to find a way to interact with people comfortably.

I found that day when I was signed up for youth sports as a kid. My parents involved me in as many sports as possible, but were obviously partial to ones they loved like basketball and soccer. I loved basketball, but like any other disobedient kid I also wanted to play ones that my parents tried to discourage, specifically football. I fell in love with it as soon as I stepped on the field, but that was no surprise as I always loved doing anything that was competitive and that got my heart rate jumping. However, there was something else about sports, especially team sports, that kept me playing long after I graduated high school and the world of organized sports; the feeling of being on a team.

This feeling of belonging, the feeling of being depended on, no matter how big or small the role of the team helped satisfy my psychological need for relatedness without me even noticing. Nothing was more rewarding than making a good play on the field or the court and having your teammates cheer you on and encourage you. I didn't need a textbook or a college level education on psychological theory to explain how good it felt to feel a sense of belonging, and to feel trusted and valued. Those were the feelings that are what ultimately kept me going to the park or to practices.

What's even better was that these experiences helped enhance my skills in other social settings beyond basketball, or whatever sport I played. I started being more vocal in class, making more friends, and I gained a new, profound confidence in myself. It wasn't even just the confidence to speak in front of people, it was much more than that. I gained a feeling of self-worth that I never had before. Sports taught me that my existence wasn't wasteful; and that alone can be the catalyst for healthy social development and your mental well-being later on into your adult life.

Not only did participation in youth sports help me to get over the initial butterflies of social interaction, but it also helped to keep me grounded in my morals and ideologies as the social pressure of the dreaded teenage years became a big factor in my life. I wanted to be accepted by my peers, but I also didn't want to be forced to do something I didn't feel comfortable with. As kids, we are confronted with these types of decisions a lot; to do what would make us look good in the eyes of our peers or to stick to the gut feeling that tells you not to do something.

Researchers from the department of Social Work and Psychology in Sweden conducted a study to see if sports could really make a difference in lowering the chances for drug use among young people. They collected data from almost 500 individuals from an island called Mauritius, which has been battling a huge drug problem amongst their youth. They asked subjects to describe their physical activity level, drug usage, education, and other questions to get a better look at how drug usage and sports interact. According to their results, sports and drug use have a negative relationship, meaning the more you do one, the less you do the other.[172]

Being active has often only been synonymous with physical and mental health, but it is time we learn about the social benefits that exercise can have in our society. Sports can help social and cognitive development in a lot of ways the classroom fails to do, and without some type of outlet to enjoy social interactions, our overall health can take a turn for the worst.

---

172 "Sports Participation And Drug Use Among Young People In Mauritius". 2019. International Journal Of Adolescence And Youth.

CHAPTER 12

AS OLD AS COMPETITION ITSELF

———

Everyone deserves feelings of self-worth no matter your background, but in a world where we are seemingly defined by our appearance before we are even given a chance to prove ourselves it becomes harder to achieve that feeling. The United States has always been regarded as the land of opportunity, but as of late there have been huge rifts between groups in our society based on their political, religious, and moral beliefs. The discrepancies in how these groups of people think have divided the nation and we are in serious need of something that has the ability to bring us back together. One of the best tools we have to solve this problem is through the power of sports.

First, we have to figure out what the underlying reasons are for the rift we see amongst different groups in society. One of the biggest contributors to our divide is the lack of equality we see in our nation. Discriminatory views of others can often put a barrier between groups of people who are more alike than they think. There is a plethora of moral reasoning that justifies the need for equal opportunity, as we are all a part of the human race and no one deserves to be treated unfairly based on appearance or due to their beliefs. The golden rule has always been "treat others as you want to be treated," but since the dawn of human existence some people have still had a problem accepting these ideologies and still selfishly hold animosity towards others due to ignorance. This discrimination only breeds more hatred into the world and if not corrected it will continue to affect the future generations of our nation, and ultimately our country's demise.

This is not a new idea as in the gospel of Matthew, written around 70 AD, it says, a "house divided against itself will not stand."[173] These words were again echoed by Former President Abraham Lincoln in the 1800s when faced with the crisis of slavery and an impending civil war. He once again explains that a country divided would never prosper and would instead be headed toward a collapse.[174]

---

173 "Bible Gateway Passage: Mark 3:25 - New International Version". 2019. Bible Gateway.
174 "House Divided" Speech By Abraham Lincoln". 2019. Abraham-lincolnonline.Org.

Knowing our history is essential to planning out our future and just like in the past we need unity to reach prosperity as a community of human beings. The power of coming together can often be seen in times of humanitarian crisis. During a major earthquake or hurricane, nations across the globe unite to support each other in their time of need. We saw this in events such as the 7.0 earthquake in Haiti or with hurricane Irma and Maria which crippled Puerto Rico, where in both cases thousands were deployed to help these communities recover after such catastrophic events[175].

Yet, there is one unifying medium that we participate in that doesn't have to do with traumatic events and suffering. As you could have guessed at this point, sports are that medium and it has the reach to not only unite a nation, but the world.

Sports have countless examples of global unity, but none are more famous than events like the World Cup or the Olympics. The United States has never been known for having the greatest men's soccer program and if we are being honest, American soccer leagues are not as popular and do not attract the level of competition that their European counterparts in England, Spain, and Italy do, which consequently means less people are watching. However, all this is thrown out the window every four years when the worldwide tournament begins. A staggering

---

175 Szalavitz, Maia, and Maia Szalavitz. 2019. "How Disasters Bring Out Our Kindness | TIME.Com". TIME.Com.

11.6 million people tuned in for the world cup final in the US compared to only 1.5 million for the MLS final. The numbers are even bigger globally as 3.5 billion people that watched the 2018 World Cup final around the world. [176]Although the United States still needs to catch up, these numbers should give you an idea of the sheer reach that sports have in general. These are not anomalies either, as other sporting events like the Olympics and Super Bowl also draw huge crowds of fans of all races, (around 30 and 100 million viewers, respectively) who come united to cheer and be a part of the action.[177]

The number of people who are watching isn't what's really important, but instead it is the way people come together to watch and cheer on whatever team they support. People from all over the world go to viewing parties, large venues, random pubs, and just about anywhere else with a working TV to watch the game or event. Oftentimes you end up watching next to someone you've never met before, but that generally awkward interaction becomes surprisingly easy as your team scores and you both jump up and down in excitement, high fiving or even embracing each other as you become over-whelmed with joy. At the moment, race, religion, gender, or any other defining category seem to cease to exist as you rally together to celebrate the success of a team that unites you.

---

176 "Super Bowl Myth Exposed: These Are Actually The Most-Watched Sporting Events". 2017. Pennlive

177 Ibid

The sense of togetherness that is built through sports not only unifies communities on the surface level, but can also have a profound impact on political policies and the state of international relations. Since its conception, the Olympics has been an outlet to unite people across the world to partake in the same event no matter their political affiliation, culture, or religious beliefs. To ensure a peaceful event, BC Iphitos, king of Elis, created a truce amongst participating nations to ensure safe travel for athletes, their families, and spectators back in the ninth century.[178] This included any nations that happened to be in conflict and was one of the first global signs that sports could be used as a peacemaking tool instead of just pitting people against each other in competition. The truce was reintroduced for the modern games in 1994 thanks to both the International Olympic Committee (IOC) and the United Nations (UN).

So, according to history we know that sports have the ability to connect and push people's differences aside, even if just for a short while, but what's more fascinating is the healing effects that sports and physical activity have on a social level.

Let's take the 2018 Winter Olympic games for example. Before then, the situation between North and South Korea was not in the best place. A long-standing history of conflict plagued

178 "The History Of The Olympic Truce". 2017. International Olympic Committee.

the region as there was consistent battles for dominance and land. The situation got even worse as North Korea built up its nuclear weapon arsenal to rival the US, who was supporting the South Korean regime. All looked to be lost, but through the power of sports a new friendship was created.

The 2018 Winter Olympic games were set to take place in South Korea and, for the first time, a symbol of better relations to come between the two neighboring countries was shown when athletes from both countries marched together during the opening ceremony for the twenty-third winter games. The Koreans didn't stop there, as they even entered a joint women's hockey team to compete against the field[179].

It is almost unimaginable that two countries on the verge of war could reconcile to a point in which they represent their countries together on a world stage. In no other situation has there been such a dramatic change of foreign relations and sports essentially worked as a method of diplomacy.

This is not the first time that sports have been able to be used as a social medicine in terms of foreign affairs either. The situation involving China and the US was a fragile one to say the least in the 1970s during the cold war. The US was fighting communism on all fronts versus Russia, while Russia

179 "Olympics Open With Koreas Marching Together, Offering Hope For Peace". 2019. Nytimes.Com

was stirring up its own problems with China due to a series of disputes over bordering lands. The US and China, although for different reasons, both saw a common enemy in Russia, and even though relations between the two countries weren't great since the Korean War where each met on the battlefield, both were open to starting a new chapter of dialogue.[180]

Just like with the 2018 Olympics, there was no better medium to open up talks other than through sports, but instead of the Olympic games the setting was the 1971 World Table Tennis Championships in Nagoya, Japan. Both countries sent their athletes, but no interactions were expected between the two, especially not ones of diplomatic significance.

All of that changed as a conversation was struck up between respected Chinese captain Zhuang Zedong and nineteen-year-old Glenn Cowan of the US on the bus to one of the table tennis events. They talked about life in their country, table tennis, and more, even though the Chinese were under strict orders to avoid confrontations with the Americans. In fact, things went so well that gifts were even exchanged as Zedong gave Cowan a silk-screen picture of the Huangshan Mountains in China and in return Cowan gave him a t-shirt with a peace symbol reading the words, "let it be," famous words of singer and peace activist John Lennon.

---

180 "How Ping-Pong Diplomacy Thawed The Cold War". 2019. HISTORY

This exchange extended beyond the tournament as the Chinese government then invited the US team to China on an expense-free trip to continue to improve their relationship in not only table tennis, but between the two national superpowers.

These athletes quickly became important diplomats for US-Chinese relations so much so that the meeting of the athletes became known as "ping-pong diplomacy." United States President at the time, Richard Nixon, was surprised even saying, "I had never expected that the China initiative would come to fruition in the form of a ping-pong team."[181] Although a surprise, both teams quickly realized the importance of what they were accomplishing. The US motto became "friendship first and competition second" and even the Chinese took the message to heart as they let the US win a few exhibition games as a sign of sportsmanship. Chinese athlete Zheng Minzhi told the New York Times, "I knew I was not only there to play, but more importantly, to achieve what cannot be achieved through proper diplomatic channels."[182]

It is not only rivalling nations that use the medicinal powers of sports, but it can sometimes be a community that is mourning after a loss or tragedy.

---

181 Ibid
182 "How Ping-Pong Diplomacy Thawed The Cold War". 2019. HISTORY

Unfortunately, in the past decade there has been a rise in the number of school shootings, terrorist attacks, and hate crimes. It's sickening that in "less than 18 years, we have already seen more deaths related to school shootings than in the whole 20th century."[183] All these events serve to divide communities and pour hatred into our nation. A special type of social healing is required to overcome such terrible events and, like many other issues, sports has the ability to help fix the problem.

One memorable way exercise helped to heal a community followed shortly after the hate crime shootings in Orlando Florida. A twenty-nine-year-old opened fire at a club in Orlando just because of their assumed sexual orientations. He killed forty-nine people and injured fifty-three more and was finally stopped after a three-hour standoff with police.[184]

Not only was the Orlando community outraged, but support was given throughout the country, especially amongst athletes. People such as LeBron James, JJ Watt, Shaquille O'Neal, and many others went to twitter and other forms of social media to let their voices be heard about their outrage over this disgusting hate crime.[185]

---

183 "Study Shows Rapid Rise In Mass School Shootings In The US". 2019. Phys.Org.
184 Orlando Shooting". 1466. Nytimes.Com.
185 Lebron Says Shooting 'Puts Things In Perspective'". 2019. ESPN.Com.

What came was another example of how sports can be used as a social medicine as many rallied together to help the community get through such a rough time. Of course, many of the local sports franchises such as the Orlando Magic, Orlando City FC, and the Tampa Bay Rays donated large sums of money to help families who were affected, but it was more than just the monetary donations that made an impact. They held commemorative nights for those who were lost in the tragedy, even having forty-nine seats reserved in the Orlando City stadium in commemoration for those who were lost. Local tournaments were held in sports such as basketball, softball, and football, and fundraising marathons were also held for the victims and relevant charities.

The MLS even allowed a stoppage time at forty-nine minutes during a soccer game for a moment of silence, a first of its kind, to honor the lives of those were taken by the attack. They didn't stop there, as they also committed to donate time and resources to local charities devoted to inclusion and equal opportunity in sports and education. For its efforts, Orlando City FC was given the Stuart Scott Enspire Award for their commitment to creating an, "innovative approach to help the disadvantaged through the power of sports."[186]

From the outside looking in, these gestures don't seem to be too impactful and although money can help ease any

186 "Response to Pulse shooting shows growth, power of soccer in U.S.". 2019. Orlandosentinel.Com.

financial issues in someone's life it cannot replace the memories of the loved one's their families have lost. It is rather the feeling of community, achieved through sports, that can help us recover from such a devastating loss. Just like being able to talk to someone and get things off your chest, or even just getting a hug from a loved one after a devastating loss can often be enough to comfort those in such a time of need.

Communities often come out in full numbers any time something like this occurs. The following Friday after the shooting the Tampa Bay Rays dedicated a benefit night for the families of the victims. Generally, the Tropicana stadium, which is one of the smallest in the MLB, isn't packed as the team supports a smaller community, but for the first time since 2008 the tarps that covered the upper deck needed to be removed to allow more people to come to the game and support the team and the community efforts.[187]

The support doesn't only come within the city that is affected, but also from all the players in the leagues and even people from all over the world. This was exemplified during the September 11th attacks on the Twin Towers in New York. Most Americans who are of age can remember exactly where they were when they first heard the news. This wasn't only a shot at the city of New York, but instead the whole nation felt the

---

187 Ibid

effects of the terrorist attack. The people of the United States decided to unite and tackle the attack straight on by donating their time and resources to the rebuilding effort.

Another magnificent thing happened that year in regards to the attack, and it had to do with the healing effect of sports. Officials urged citizens to go back to their daily lives to try to get things back to normal, and the New York Yankees would follow suit as they were in position for a shot at the World Series. Many thought the impact of the attack could leave the city and the players too distraught to do damage in the playoffs, but regardless of the negative speculation surrounding them, the Yankees remained focused on winning, and did just that.

Playing with a renewed sense of passion and pride, the Yankees reached the 2001 World Series filling fans and the city with hope and allowed them to focus on the magic of sports instead of the terrible events that just occurred. Just as the whole nation felt the attacks of September 11th, so did their hearts also fill as the Yankees showed their perseverance during such a difficult time. It is important to note that generally fans of other teams were not too fond of the Yankees, but famous actor Billy Elliot even says, "for the first time in, I think the history of baseball, people around the country were pulling for the Yankees to win."[188]

---

188 "How Major League Baseball Responded To 9/11". 2011. Sbnation.Com

The Yankees went on to lose that World Series, but what it did for the city of New York and the country in general is something that should not be underrated. Through sports, the Yankees took away the sad and gloomy cloud that haunted New York, giving them pride and healing their minds in a time where they needed it most.

The use of sports for this purpose is not talked about enough and the healing power of sports is more common than what is displayed to the public. Other examples are the Boston bombings which took place during the annual Boston marathon and also devastated the nation. Again, the Boston sports teams, natives, and people around the states united together to mourn and support each other after a terrible event. Many teams including the Bruins, Red Sox, and the Celtics began wearing #BostonStrong shirts for warm ups and many other teams and fans also began to wear and use the hashtag to support the people of Boston, getting them through another difficult time.[189]

Natural disasters also bring upon the unifying power of sports. For example, the New Orleans community following Hurricane Katrina and the actions of the New Orleans Saints or the Houston and Costal Texas Communities following Hurricane Harvey and the response by the multiple major sports

189 "Sports & Healing: How Boston Teams Helped City Heal After Marathon Tragedy". 2014. CBS Boston.

franchise teams in Texas in 2017. Both cases showed sports teams hosting benefit nights, donating time and resources to provide shelter, food, and water, and much more.[190]

In all these instances, whether it be a national disasters, terrorist attack, or other type of tragedy, sports help to distract people of the community from the chaos and sadness that they face, and turn their attention to something more positive. No matter the color of your skin, religious beliefs, cultural background, or whatever else makes you different, we can all find love and unity through the power of sports.

190 Szalavitz, Maia, and Maia Szalavitz. 2019. "How Disasters Bring Out Our Kindness | TIME.Com". TIME.Com.

CHAPTER 13

FINDING A COMMON GROUND

———

The power of sports or exercise is one that unites. It brings people from different backgrounds together to reach a common goal, while providing an extensive list of health benefits for everyone who partakes. The amazing thing that sport or other types of exercise done with a group or a partner has to offer is that the sense of comradery is not just confined to the game itself. You continue to foster stronger relationships with teammates, coaches, and parents as you share meals, car rides, and just chat on the sideline together. Overall, sports have the ability to create a sense of community amongst a diverse group of people, the little things in this world have the power to do. This helps to build new perspectives on cultural backgrounds and different ways of life that an individual may not have experienced before, which ultimately creates a feeling of empathy that can help bring people closer, even turning friends into family.

I can relate to that feeling firsthand, as my teammates and coaches from youth and high school sports were part of my extended family. We spent so much time together laughing, working, and just being around each other that bonding with each other was inevitable. Even in times where any of my teammates were going through a tough time with their families, they always knew that when they were with the team, they had another place to call home.

These feelings allow us to begin to care more for each other and look out for one another, and by doing that we can make the world a better place. It might sound cliché, but sports are one of the only mechanisms that can actually accomplish that goal. In a lot of ways, sports are like a super glue that binds us together no matter where we are from or what we are made of; the bond you build through physical activity is one as strong as a real family bond.

What's even more amazing is that sports don't require a specific language. In fact, in sports sometimes you don't need any words at all and yet everyone can be on the same page. Oftentimes, I would play basketball at the park in New York and there were always people from all walks of life trying to play pick-up. Some of these people spoke English as their second language and some didn't even speak it at all, but once they stepped onto the court, this feeling of familiarity always seemed to overcome our team. A lot of sports have a universal language that you can learn just by playing enough. Oftentimes, my teammates and I would cut, or switch defenders without even having to communicate with each other in our own languages. No one ever gave anybody specific directions, but everyone just kind of knew how to play off each other.

The rules are often the same for sports no matter where in the world you are, so there are always opportunities to interact with different types of people on a common ground no matter what sport or physical activity it may be. Sports allow us to meet in a place where there is no "right" political affiliation, a place where it doesn't matter what religion or race you are, but instead help us free our minds of all the social constructs that restrict our minds and enjoy the company of others while achieving the bonus of benefiting our bodies at the same time.

This type of acceptance is one that should be carried over into our everyday lives. We should let sports be the model for how to structure a cohesive society where everyone plays a part and is of equal value.

Growing up, I was personally affected by this, as without sports I don't know where I would be socially. I longed desperately to fit in and make friends and it wasn't until I joined youth sports that I truly found the group that I would call my best friends for the rest of my life. It was for the same reasons I could go to a park and instantly be on the same page with someone on the basketball court or the soccer field, sports connect people in impactful ways. The more sports I played, the less I would feel like I was an outsider. Instead I felt like part of a family, someone who mattered; someone who was equal.

Before all the positive things that come from these types of activities can happen, they have to be available first. For that to happen, we have to address a rising problem in our nation and around the globe, which is that people of lower socioeconomic status (SES) generally have less access to team sports leagues and facilities for physical activity, and as a result also participate in physical activity less.[191]

Now, although I you don't need any equipment to be physically active the chance that a person becomes and stays active can be influenced by the amount of resources they have around them. Joining youth sports leagues or joining private gyms often cost money and sometimes families cannot afford to tackle the extra payments associated with it. Not

---

191 Giles-Corti, B. 2002. "Socioeconomic Status Differences In Recreational Physical Activity Levels And Real And Perceived Access To A Supportive Physical Environment". Preventive Medicine 35

only that, but sometimes, the school systems that lower SES community members are enrolled in also do not have the proper funding to provide quality physical education and the youth suffers because of it.[192]

These factors and more contribute to the disparity we see between physical activity for lower SES communities versus ones who have a higher status. Research surveys done by the Centers for Disease Control (CDC) and the physical activity guidelines gathered information on 30,000 individuals from across the nation from all different age ranges. They found that compared to Caucasians, African Americans and Hispanics get 37 percent and 18 percent less amount of nonwork physical activity than their fellow citizens.[193] [194]

As we are continuing to learn, doing less movement leads to higher chances for a plethora of diseases and even premature mortality. As you limit a person's access to opportunities to be physically active, you also increase the risk that they are more sedentary, obese, and many other associated diseases. So, it only makes sense that the

192 Bowser J, et al. 2019. "Disparities In Fitness And Physical Activity Among Children. - Pubmed - NCBI

193 Douglas et al.1983. "Differences Among Black, Hispanic, And White People In Knowledge About Long-Term Care Services". Health Care Financing Review 5

194 "Fact Sheet: Health Disparities By Race And Ethnicity". 2010. Center For American Progress.

CDC reports that a higher percentage of African American and Hispanics suffer from obesity, 46.8 percent and 47 percent respectively, compared to the national average of 39.8 percent.[195] Obesity is linked with higher chances for cardiovascular diseases, diabetes, and many others that can impair your quality of life. For this reason, we must look to see why these rates are higher in our lower SES communities and how we can lower these percentages for everyone in the nation.

Things do start to make sense as we dive deeper into the issue and look more closely at the data. The CDC has released reports and analysis that show evidence to two major contributors to this gap in physical activity between these demographics: education and income.

The numbers suggest that the higher your education level, the less likely you are to become obese. Compared to people who graduated college, nongraduates were found to be 12 percent more likely to suffer from obesity for men and 13 percent for women. The percentage dropped even lower when compared to those who did not complete high school to those who finished college by the time they reached adulthood.[196]

195 "Adult Obesity Facts | Overweight & Obesity | CDC". 2019. Cdc.Gov
196 Yu, Yan. 2011. "Educational Differences In Obesity In The United States: A Closer Look At The Trends". Obesity 20

The story for income becomes a little more complicated when examining the overall trends. Generally, we would expect to see an increase in the amount of physical activity a person participates in as their income increases; however, that is only observed in women, as male rates of obesity are actually highest in high-income males. Some hypothesize that it is because African American and Hispanic males often work more labor intensive jobs at the low-income categorization. Others point to the fact that having a higher income allows you to have things to convenience your life including a car, which can often eliminate a large portion of physical activity from daily lives.

Another shocking statistic is that women are at a higher risk of obesity compared to men, specifically minority women. According to government figures, nearly 50 percent of African American women over age twenty are overweight or obese, compared with 33 percent of white women and 43 percent of Hispanic women. Again, there seems to be a consistent imbalance in the obesity rates between different populations. Calling one or two of these statistics a coincidence is understandable, but the more you see the data, the more it tells you that those in more disadvantaged communities lack access to physical activity facilities such as parks and fields that take away opportunities that most of us take for granted.[197]

---

197 "Adult Obesity Facts | Overweight & Obesity | CDC". 2019. Cdc.Gov.

As we strive to be a more balanced and unified country, one thing that we can do is create more opportunities in communities for exercise. This can be accomplished by building parks and fields no matter how small, or even just by making sure sidewalks are well kept so the community becomes walkable. Schools will play a big role through physical education to not only teach the youth important life skills while playing, but also teach them about the benefits that physical activity has to offer.

There are other reasons to stop the increase in obesity rates as well, not only for minorities, but for all the people in the country, and that reason is money.

When someone gets sick, it takes a certain amount of cost to get the resources to heal them. The more people that get injured, or get sick, the more money that is needed to heal those individuals that could have been allocated somewhere else. Of course, it is imperative to take care of everyone no matter what disease they are faced with, but if there is a way to decrease the prevalence of these diseases and, therefore, saving every tax paying citizen money, then why wouldn't we?

We aren't playing with chump change here either, as obesity accounted for $147 billion in 2008 in total costs to healthcare and the amount of people with obesity has only increased since then. As we learned, obesity can increase your risk for other diseases which can also be costly, as diabetes is responsible for costing $190.5 billion in annual spending.[198] With these diseases and many others being such a financial burden on our healthcare system we need to begin prioritizing interventions to reduce them.

These numbers aren't just things that we can leave for the government to handle, as the lack of physical activity affects us on a very personal level financially as well. Compared to nonobese individuals "per capita medical spending for obese individuals is $1,429 higher per year, or roughly 42 percent higher."[199]

This added cost can come in many forms, but it certainly is not a light load, especially when considering not everyone is in a financially stable situation and that extra $1,400 can go towards groceries, rent, tutors, or other important necessities. For this reason, it is especially important to try to eliminate gaps in the amount of physical activity and education we see amongst the people of lower SES in our nation as if they are faced with not only the problem of not having the income to expend the extra amount of money on health care costs, but also are at a higher risk for these health problems. This double dipping effect can often lead families in a cycle from

198 "Adult Obesity Causes & Consequences | Overweight & Obesity | CDC". 2019. Cdc.Gov.

199 "Economic Costs". 2012. Obesity Prevention Source.

which they cannot recover, only making their problems and the overall disadvantage they are placed at worse.

Major economic catastrophes such as the 2008 financial recession can also have a profound effect on the amount of people who are at added risk for obesity and other linked diseases. The John Hopkins school of public health found that not only did wage gap increase and access to healthcare become harder, but the risk of acquiring obesity also increased disproportionately for minorities when compared to the national averages. "American Indians and Pacific Islanders were 22 percent more likely to become obese as unemployment rose. Among black children, obesity risk ticked up 1.6 percentage points for each single digit increase in unemployment." [200]

So, when it comes to inequality, we clearly see a discrepancy between different subpopulations regarding the average amount of physical activity they get and their chances for acquiring certain diseases. It is easy to think that the problem is too complex and far gone to uproot, but luckily for all of us there is still hope to solve these issues and it may not be as difficult as fixing the divide in America.

In fact, the only thing we need to get people to do to fix this problem, like the solution to every other problem presented

200 "Rise In Unemployment During Recession Linked To Weight Gain In Children". 2016. The Hub.

in this book is to get moving. Government research for the CDC have found, "that once initial engagement in physical activity is established, socioeconomic status ceases to be a critical determinant for engagement in exercise and overall movement."[201] It's like they always say, "the first step is always the hardest," and that rains true here, as once you begin an exercise regimen it is much easier to stay active and the risk of obesity and other diseases begin to decrease back to a healthy baseline.

Hope is not lost and that is what is important to remember and there are many ways to go about increasing access to physical activity in underprivileged communities. Through the money that could be saved in healthcare if the American population increase their physical activity levels or through the reallocations of other funding more low-cost recreation facilities, free camps or exercise classes can be established, which can help lower the physical activity inequality gap.

Thousands of corporations and nonprofits that are striving to accomplish this mission as well, including RISE (Ross Initiative in Sports for Equality), and Global Crossover, an organization that builds basketball courts in disadvantaged communities.[202] Both not-for-profit organizations want to

---

201 "Prevalence of Obesity Among Adults and Youth: United States, 2015–2016" 2019. Cdc.Gov
202 " RISE To Win". 2019. Risetowin.Org.

use sports to bridge the social inequality gap and provide communities with the tools to build a healthy life.

During an interview, the co-president of Global Crossover said that, "sports are the key to bringing people together and forming tight community bonds. I'll never forget growing so close with my teammates and the happiness it brought me, so our team is just trying to provide that same happiness to communities who otherwise wouldn't be able to. I've honestly never seen anything else consistently bring group of different people together so closely other than sport."

Whether it be personal experiences or if you are viewing it from the sideline, there is no questioning the unifying ability that sports have on a community.

CHAPTER 14

WE COULD LEARN A THING OR TWO

——

We face many challenges as an international community regarding health and equality. Along with the basic human needs of food, water, and shelter, the ability to be healthy should also be considered as a basic human right. Without the knowledge and tools to set yourself up for the future your body, it could be headed down the wrong path, and getting one of the many conditions we have discussed in this book is more likely. One of the only ways to prevent your quality of life from being impacted is by being properly educated on how to be healthy both mentally and physically, as well as provide access to equipment and facilities that will encourage participation in physical activity of all types for the youth, and for adults too.

Education has always been the key to making a change in society and it's evident once you take a look at history. Education was one of the key pillars of democracy, as it wasn't until people had the knowledge to elect capable leaders that they were allowed to participate in such important things such as government structure. As Franklin D. Roosevelt said, "Democracy cannot succeed unless those who express their choice are prepared to choose wisely. The real safeguard of democracy, therefore, is education."[203]

Education has also brought about social change through social justice leaders who have preached its importance for decades. The great Nelson Mandela was quoted saying, "Education is the most powerful weapon which you can use to change the world,"[204] and Malcolm X has also been quoted saying that, "Education is the passport to the future, for tomorrow belongs to those who prepare for it today."[205] Through education people were finally able to understand that we are all made equal and that realization began the chain reaction to more opportunity for those who once were oppressed. Education has the power to change how we think.

---

203 Quality Public Education + Dialogue = Democracy". 2019. Huffpost.Com

204 Arne Duncan, U.S. Secretary of Education. 2019. " Education: The Most Powerful Weapon For Changing The World | USAID Impact ". Blog.Usaid.Gov.

205 The Open Doors" 2019. Lonestar.Edu.

Of course, besides major social changes, education has also allowed us to make healthy changes in our lives. Once upon a time, people thought it was alright to smoke a pack of cigarettes a day. That all changed as more research began to be conducted on the cancer-causing risk factors associated with smoking. Once the evidence became concrete enough, a national epidemic to educate people on the adverse health effects of cigarettes followed soon after, ensuring that children were properly educated about their effects in school. Soon enough, smoking cigarettes began to be universally known as being terrible for your health and with a combination of higher taxes being placed on tobacco, cigarette sales have continued to decrease, lowering 3.5 percent since 2016.[206]

So, as we've done repeatedly throughout history to make a change, we need to start by using education, but just like in other facets of American life, things don't always add up equally. People with a higher socioeconomic status (SES) generally have better physical education opportunities during school hours. This is due to many interconnected factors, but one of the main causes of this problem that these low SES schools face is that they lack proper funding to hire enough physical education (PE) teachers.

---

206 "Economic Report of the President" 2016. Govinfo.Gov

A survey was done on ninety-seven different elementary schools where the principle and PE teachers would answer questions on a survey related to their physical education experiences. The study found that low SES schools were less likely to have enough PE teachers to proficiently watch all the kids for a given school. The absence of a more personable physical education would be found to hinder the amount of physical activity kids accomplish during PE hours by about four and a half minutes of moderate or vigorous physical activity (MVPA). [207]Although these four and a half minutes seem insignificant, they add up when combined for weekly totals, and in an already long school day, students need to squeeze in as many extra minutes as possible to make their weekly requirements.

For this reason, it is not only important to make sure that the appropriate amount of PE teachers are hired, it is also important that normal subject teachers be trained in some type of physical education training to allow as much activity as possible for students throughout the day, and consequently a better learning environment. This survey showed that more low and moderate SES elementary schools need PE teachers to reduce disparities in school physical activity opportunities, but more importantly that PE time needs

207 Carlson et al. 2014. "Socioeconomic Disparities In Elementary School Practices And Children's Physical Activity During School". American Journal Of Health Promotion 28

to be supplemented by classroom teachers or other staff to meet guidelines.[208]

Many people ask "why is PE so important in the first place?" and "aren't there more important things to do with our money than make gym class better for kids?" Well, we know that kids should strive to get an hour of physical activity every day. This helps them develop both cognitively, socially, and also helps them focus better throughout the day so they can learn more.

A study conducted by researchers at the University of Illinois department of kinesiology ran an experiment on twenty kids in primary school to see how their brains would work after a twenty-minute walk. They assessed their cardiovascular and cognitive function shortly after and found that the exercise helped improve their attention and, consequently, improved their test scores.[209]

PE provides health benefits by giving students that extra few minutes of exercise, while helping them fine tune their focus for the rest of the day. Without PE, students would be spending a majority of their day stuck sitting, which can end up doing more harm than good to their health.

---

208 Ibid
209 "Move It, Move It: How Physical Activity At School Helps The Mind (As Well As The Body)". 2018. The Conversation.

Still, many people do not believe the impact that PE can have on students. They say too many kids are sitting on the side during PE class, or make excuses like being sick to get out of gym class for the day. Sometimes, even parents get involved giving their children notes that excuse them from PE. For this reason, we must not only educate the youth, but also the parents and teachers to encourage them to be as physically active as possible throughout the day, instead of just letting kids slide.

Researchers at the UC Berkeley Center for Weight and Health wanted to put this debate to an end and prove the advantages of a great PE program and the effect it can have on students. They surveyed over 9,000 ninth and tenth grade students asking them questions on their physical activity levels and their PE curriculum. After examining all the data, the researchers found that "engaging in at least 20 minutes of exercise during PE class was significantly associated with both shorter mile times and lower body mass index scores."[210] This led them to conclude that PE was by far the most significant predictor of students' fitness and was the only variable associated with improved weight status that they could find that had a strong correlation associated with it.

So, the importance of PE in schools should not be underestimated, as it is an essential component to building a

---

210 "Physical Education Key To Improving Health In Low-Income Adolescents". 2009. | UC San Francisco.

foundation to build healthy habits that will last into adulthood. Yet, so many students still hate PE class. A look at a 2007 to 2011 state mandated PE initiative in Texas gives a closer look as to why that is the case. Schools were given $10,000 under the Fitness Now program to enforce a mandatory thirty minutes of PE every school day. The money would go toward new equipment such as jump ropes, stopwatches, and anything that could be used during gym class. Punishment would be given to those who skipped PE in the form of sitting out at recess or free time.

Surprisingly, the intervention proved to be detrimental to the students PE experience, as researchers following the intervention found a 16 percent increase in the number of disciplinary actions for each student. The study also found that the proportion of misbehaved students went up by more than 7 percent during PE class[211].

One reason for this increase could be that PE class is often structured in a way to get students to meet certain criteria in terms of things like how fast they can run a mile or how many sit-ups or push-ups they can do. This puts the emphasis of exercise too much on performance rather than health. Students are also forced to learn basic skills for every sport

211 Von Hippel et al. 2015. "The Effects Of School Physical Education Grants On Obesity, Fitness, And Academic Achievement". Preventive Medicine

in the curriculum, even when they have no interest in them. This creates a very boring gym class environment for some and makes these kids not want to attend class or misbehave to get out of having to participate.

A solution for this can be offering multiple types of gym classes so students can have more autonomy over the types of activities they participate in and, therefore, be more likely to be invested in their health. This is becoming a popular tactic and was something Athletic Director of the Smithtown Central School District, Patrick Smith, wanted to make sure to incorporate when making the structure for PE in his high schools. He believes by offering more choices to students their MVPA will also increase and the things they learn in class will stick with them throughout their lives.

As an alumnus of Smithtown East High School, I can strongly attest to how much this works. My classmates who loved to play competitive sports such as basketball, softball, volleyball, and others would join the team sports class and the games were often competitive, yet good-spirited, as almost everyone in the class would look forward to gym instead of agonizing over it. For those who didn't like team sports other classes such as yoga, weightlifting, or dancing were also offered in which students could pick their favorite activity and stick with it for a year.

Another issue with the current PE system is that it categorizes students based on their fitness tests and labels certain students as better than others instead of making the focus on individual improvement. This allows bullying to manifest itself especially in places that lack supervision such as gym locker rooms. Students who get bullied because their fitness test results aren't as high as their peers, will be less likely to want to come back to gym class because all it does is make them feel inferior.

It is hardly fair to judge kids who are still in the prime of their developmental years to have to perform a particular amount of certain exercise, and just like in the Fitness Now program in Texas, kids will begin to disobey just because they are not happy with the way things are set up.

For this reason, it is imperative that we shift the structure of PE to something they are looking forward to, and something that will focus on personal achievement rather than comparative performance. The more enjoyment students find from PE classes, the more likely they are to participate in the activities in the class, and the more likely they are to carry these skills throughout their lives.

PE class, if organized correctly, can be a fantastic way to teach students about the importance of physical activity, but generally, kids do not have gym class every day, instead they have it every other day switching off with some other elective, or even have it just twice a week. This leaves kids to be stuck in a chair for a majority of the day which can hinder their ability to learn. For this reason, many schools have begun to encourage physical activity during their main subject classes as well.

Ideas such as taking a few minutes to walk around and stretch are often utilized to give students the break they need to stay focused and on task. One of the best ways to encourage movement throughout the day is through providing some type of recess, but with new focuses on education, recess availability has taken a hit.

It's no secret that the United States has fallen behind the rest of the world in terms of education. The US is currently seventeenth in education, seventh in literacy, thirtieth in math, and nineteenth in the sciences.[212] This is shocking for the self-proclaimed "greatest country in the world," and as a result these rankings have influenced US agenda on education proficiency.

Focusing on getting our students smarter is a good thing, but it should not be at the expense of one's health as many schools, especially ones that have to choose between hiring

212 "The US Was Once A Leader For Healthcare And Education — Now It Ranks 27Th In The World". 2019. Business Insider

a science teacher or a recess monitor, have begun to cut back on recess time to help boost scores.

The Center on Education Policy at the George Washington University found that "62% of school districts had increased the amount of time spent on English language arts or math in elementary schools since 2001,"[213] and recess has been cut back as a result. According to the 2016 Shape of the Nation report, just 16 percent of states require elementary schools to provide daily recess, even though the CDC reports that, "there is substantial evidence that physical activity can help improve academic achievement, including grades and standardized test scores." [214]

Instead of taking away recess, school districts should focus on making core curriculum more efficient, as there is overwhelming data that suggests that recess actually helps learning. Lawmakers are finally starting to catch on as new bills in states such as Florida and New York have proposed outlawing teachers from withholding recess as a form of punishment, as it has been proven to make things even worse.[215]

All evidence points to the importance of physical activity in the productivity of our youth in schools whether that be through

---

213 " Center On Education Policy". 2019. Cep-Dc.Org
214 "Shape of the Nation" 2019. Shapeamerica.Org.
215 Portner, Jessica. 2019. " 46 States Mandate P.E., But Only Four Require In All Grades - Education Week". Edweek.Org

PE, recess, or regularly scheduled breaks during the school day. The education of physical activity and health should be treated as something that is just as important as any other subject taught in school, and in my opinion, it should be one of the most important things emphasized to the kids. We often learn a very broad overview of each subject, but many complain about how they, "will never use this information in their lives." Generally, they are not wrong and although having a good base of knowledge is important for building well-rounded people, shouldn't it be more pressing that we teach our youth skills that they will use 100 percent of their lives? The key here is finding the balance between it all without taking away from an important component of learning.

Physical activity in schools through sports can also encourage equality between peers by creating vital community bonds and spurring social interactions from those who would generally not seek it. By providing these opportunities to all the students of our nation, we can strive to build a healthier and more accepting world, and by accomplishing that, our test scores and rankings will follow suit.

The powers of exercise are limitless. It not only heals an individual's body, but through sports and being active we can heal the nation as well. Education is the catalyst for starting a revolution in future generations and it is our responsibility to learn about the body-changing effects of exercise, implement them in our own lives, then pass our knowledge to the youth, who will as a result live healthier lives and continue to expand and discover even more benefits that being active can offer us.

APPENDIX

———

INTRO

1. "NVSS - Mortality Data". 2019. *Cdc.Gov.* Accessed October 10 2019.

2. Santhanam, Laura, and Laura Santhanam. 2018. "American Life Expectancy Has Dropped Again. Here's Why". *PBS Newshour.* Accessed October 10 2019.

3. "Historical - Centers For Medicare & Medicaid Services". 2019. *Cms.Gov.* Accessed October 10 2019

4. "How Does Health Spending In The U.S. Compare To Other Countries? - Peterson-Kaiser Health System Tracker". 2019. *Peterson-Kaiser Health System Tracker.* Accessed October 10 2019

5. "Economic Costs Of Obesity | Healthy Communities For A Healthy Future". 2019. *Healthycommunitieshealthyfuture.Org.*

6. "Childhood Obesity Facts | Overweight & Obesity | CDC". 2019. *Cdc.Gov.*

7. "Faststats-Leading Causes of Death". 2019. *Cdc.Gov.* Accessed October 11 2019.

8. "Faststats-Exercise or Physical Activity". 2019. *Cdc.Gov.* Accessed October 11 2019.

9. 2019. *Disabilitycompendium.Org*. Accessed October 11 2019. https://disabilitycompendium.org/sites/default/files/user-uploads/2017_AnnualReport_2017_FINAL.pdf.

10. "Physical Activity Guidelines for Americans 2nd Edition". *Health.Gov*. Accessed October 11 2019. https://health.gov/paguidelines/second-edition/pdf/Physical_Activity_Guidelines_2nd_edition.pdf.

11. Tipton, Charles M. 2014. "The History Of "Exercise Is Medicine" In Ancient Civilizations". *Advances In Physiology Education* 38 (2): 109-117. American Physiological Society. doi:10.1152/advan.00136.2013.

12. "The Most Popular 2019 New Year's Resolutions | Vitagene". 2018. *Vitagene*. Accessed October 11 2019. https://vitagene.com/blog/most-popular-2019-new-years-resolution/.

13. Naci, H., and J. P. A. Ioannidis. 2013. "Comparative Effectiveness Of Exercise And Drug Interventions On Mortality Outcomes: Metaepidemiological Study". *BMJ* 347 (oct01 1): f5577-f5577. BMJ. doi:10.1136/bmj.f5577.

14. Publishing, Harvard. 2019. "What We Do—And Don't—Know About Exercise - Harvard Health". *Harvard Health*. Accessed October 11 2019. https://www.health.harvard.edu/staying-healthy/what-we-do-and-dont-know-about-exercise.

15. "Award Program Information". 2012. *HHS.Gov*. Accessed October 11 2019. https://www.hhs.gov/fitness/programs-and-awards/presidents-challenge/index.html.

16. "Incidence Of Childhood Obesity In The United States | NEJM". 2019. *New England Journal Of Medicine*. Accessed October 11 2019. https://www.nejm.org/doi/full/10.1056/NEJMoa1309753.

17. "Sports Participation And Drug Use Among Young People In Mauritius". 2019. *International Journal Of Adolescence And Youth*. https://www.tandfonline.com/doi/full/10.1080/02673843.2017.1325756.

18. "Benefits Of Regular Exercise - Imagine Health". 2019. *Imagine Health*. Accessed October 11 2019. http://imaginehealth.ie/benefits-regular-exercise/

19. "Home Food Availability, Parental Dietary Intake, And Familial Eating Habits Influence The Diet Quality Of Urban Hispanic Children | Childhood Obesity".

20. Branen, Laurel, and Janice Fletcher. 1999. "Comparison Of College Students' Current Eating Habits And Recollections Of Their Childhood Food Practices". *Journal Of Nutrition Education* 31 (6): 304-310. Elsevier BV. doi:10.1016/s0022-3182(99)70483-8.

21. "Parental Influence On Children's Oral Health-Related Behavior". 2019. *Acta Odontologica Scandinavica.* https://www.tandfonline.com/doi/full/10.1080/00016350600714498.

22. Fuemmeler, Bernard F, Cheryl B Anderson, and Louise C Mâsse. 2011. "Parent-Child Relationship Of Directly Measured Physical Activity". *International Journal Of Behavioral Nutrition And Physical Activity* 8 (1): 17. Springer Nature. doi:10.1186/1479-5868-8-17.

23. Loprinzi, Paul D., and Stewart G. Trost. 2010. "Parental Influences On Physical Activity Behavior In Preschool Children". *Preventive Medicine* 50 (3): 129-133. Elsevier BV. doi:10.1016/j.ypmed.2009.11.010.

24. Dominique Gummelt, PhD. 2015. "Physical Activity Vs. Exercise: What'S The Difference?". *Acefitness.Org.* Accessed October 11 2019. https://www.acefitness.org/education-and-resources/lifestyle/blog/5460/physical-activity-vs-exercise-what-s-the-difference.

25. "Definition Of DOCTOR". 2019. *Merriam-Webster.Com.* Accessed October 11 2019. https://www.merriam-webster.com/dictionary/doctor.

26. "How I Lost 100 Lbs Swimming 4X/Week | (Michael Allon) #Askaswimpro Show". 2019. *Youtube.* Accessed October 11 2019. https://www.youtube.com/watch?v=452JBIgMatE&t=1228s.

EXERCISE PRESCRIPTION

27. Thomas, Sue. 2011. "The Power Of Physical Therapy: One Student's Story Of Brain Injury And Recovery". *Mlive.Com.* https://www.mlive.com/living/grand-rapids/2011/05/the_power_of_physical_therapy.html.

28. Shaik, AbdulRahim, and ArakkalManiyat Shemjaz. 2014. "The Rise Of Physical Therapy: A History In Footsteps". *Archives Of Medicine And Health Sciences* 2 (2): 257. Medknow. doi:10.4103/2321-4848.144367.

29. American Physical Therapy Association. 2019. "About Physical Therapist (PT) Careers". *Apta.Org*. http://www.apta.org/ptcareers/overview/.

30. Finder, Chuck, and Anthony Delitto. 2019. "Physical Therapy, Surgery Produce Same Results For Spinal Stenosis In Older Patients | Pitt Chronicle | University Of Pittsburgh". *Chronicle.Pitt.Edu*. https://www.chronicle.pitt.edu/story/physical-therapy-surgery-produce-same-results-spinal-stenosis-older-patients.

31. "Physical Activity Guidelines for Americans 2nd Edition". *Health.Gov*. Accessed October 11 2019. https://health.gov/paguidelines/second-edition/pdf/Physical_Activity_Guidelines_2nd_edition.pdf.

32. Hirsch, Mark A., Erwin E. H. van Wegen, Mark A. Newman, and Patricia C. Heyn. 2018. "Exercise-Induced Increase In Brain-Derived Neurotrophic Factor In Human Parkinson's Disease: A Systematic Review And Meta-Analysis". *Translational Neurodegeneration* 7 (1). Springer Nature. doi:10.1186/s40035-018-0112-1.

33. "VIDEO REPLAY: Dr. Liz Joy Gives 2019 Blyth Lecture | Department Of Exercise And Sport Science". 2019. *Exss.Unc.Edu*. Accessed October 11 2019. https://exss.unc.edu/2019/04/video-replay-dr-liz-joy-gives-2019-blyth-lecture/.

34. Church, T. S., Y. J. Cheng, C. P. Earnest, C. E. Barlow, L. W. Gibbons, E. L. Priest, and S. N. Blair. 2003. "Exercise Capacity And Body Composition As Predictors Of Mortality Among Men With Diabetes". *Diabetes Care* 27 (1): 83-88. American Diabetes Association. doi:10.2337/diacare.27.1.83.

THE SITTING DISEASE

35. Matthews, C. E., K. Y. Chen, P. S. Freedson, M. S. Buchowski, B. M. Beech, R. R. Pate, and R. P. Troiano. 2008. "Amount Of Time Spent In Sedentary Behaviors In The United States, 2003-2004". *American Journal Of Epidemiology* 167 (7): 875-881. Oxford University Press (OUP). doi:10.1093/aje/kwm390.

36. Jetté M, et al. 2019. "Metabolic Equivalents (METS) In Exercise Testing, Exercise Prescription, And Evaluation Of Functional Capacity. - Pubmed - NCBI ". *Ncbi.Nlm.Nih.Gov*. Accessed October 11 2019. https://www.ncbi.nlm.nih.gov/pubmed/2204507.

37. McCall, Pete. 2017. "5 Things To Know About Metabolic Equivalents". *Acefitness.Org*. Accessed October 11 2019. https://www.acefitness.org/education-and-resources/professional/expert-articles/6434/5-things-to-know-about-metabolic-equivalents.

38. Keadle, Sarah K., Steven C. Moore, Joshua N. Sampson, Qian Xiao, Demetrius Albanes, and Charles E. Matthews. 2015. "Causes Of Death Associated With Prolonged TV Viewing". *American Journal Of Preventive Medicine* 49 (6): 811-821. Elsevier BV. doi:10.1016/j.amepre.2015.05.023.

39. HEALTH, PHYSICAL. 2010. "PHYSICAL ACTIVITY FOR HEALTH". *World Health Organization*. https://www.ncbi.nlm.nih.gov/books/NBK305049/#targetText=Physical%20inactivity%20has%20been%20identified,of%20global%20mortality%20(1).

40. "Nutrition And Health Are Closely Related - 2015-2020 Dietary Guidelines - Health.Gov". 2019. *Health.Gov*. Accessed October 12 2019. https://health.gov/dietaryguidelines/2015/guidelines/introduction/nutrition-and-health-are-closely-related/#targetText=About%20half%20of%20all%20American,cancers%2C%20and%20poor%20bone%20health.

41. "Scientific Report" 2019. *Health.Gov*. Accessed October 12 2019. https://health.gov/paguidelines/second-edition/report/pdf/PAG_Advisory_Committee_Report.pdf.

42. "The Facts Behind 'Sitting Disease' And Living Sedentary | Juststand.Org". 2019. *Juststand.Org*. Accessed October 12 2019. https://www.juststand.org/the-facts/.

43. Gao, Lan, Anna Flego, David W Dunstan, Elisabeth AH Winkler, Genevieve N Healy, Elizabeth G Eakin, and Lisa Willenberg et al. 2018. "Economic Evaluation Of A Randomized Controlled Trial Of An Intervention To Reduce Office Workers' Sitting Time: The "Stand Up Victoria" Trial". *Scandinavian Journal Of Work, Environment & Health* 44 (5): 503-511. Scandinavian Journal of Work, Environment and Health. doi:10.5271/sjweh.3740.

44. "Inadequate Physical Activity and Health Care Expenditures in the United States" 2019. *Cdc.Gov*. Accessed October 12 2019. https://www.cdc.gov/nccdphp/dnpao/docs/carlson-physical-activity-and-healthcare-expenditures-final-508tagged.pdf.

45. "How Much Is 117 Billion? (How Much Is 117,000,000,000?)". 2019. *Researchmaniacs.Com*. Accessed October 12 2019. https://researchmaniacs.com/Numbers/Billions/How-much-is-117-billion.html.

46. EL, Ryan. 2019. "Self-Determination Theory And The Facilitation Of Intrinsic Motivation, Social Development, And Well-Being. - Pubmed - NCBI ". *Ncbi.Nlm.Nih.Gov.* Accessed October 12 2019. https://www.ncbi. nlm.nih.gov/pubmed/11392867.

47. Duncan, Lindsay R, Craig R Hall, Philip M Wilson, and Jenny O. 2010. "Exercise Motivation: A Cross-Sectional Analysis Examining Its Relationships With Frequency, Intensity, And Duration Of Exercise". *International Journal Of Behavioral Nutrition And Physical Activity* 7 (1): 7. Springer Nature. doi:10.1186/1479-5868-7-7.

48. White, Daniel K., Catrine Tudor-Locke, Yuqing Zhang, Roger Fielding, Michael LaValley, David T. Felson, and K. Douglas Gross et al. 2014. "Daily Walking And The Risk Of Incident Functional Limitation In Knee Osteoarthritis: An Observational Study". *Arthritis Care & Research* 66 (9): 1328-1336. Wiley. doi:10.1002/acr.22362.

49. "Fall Prevention Stats". 2019. *Ncoa.Org.* Accessed October 12. https://www. ncoa.org/news/resources-for-reporters/get-the-facts/falls-prevention-facts/.

50. "Physical Activity Guidelines for Americans 2nd Edition". *Health.Gov.* Accessed October 11 2019. https://health.gov/paguidelines/second-edition/ pdf/Physical_Activity_Guidelines_2nd_edition.pdf.

51. "Important Facts About Falls | Home And Recreational Safety | CDC Injury Center". 2019. *Cdc.Gov.* Accessed October 12 2019. https://www.cdc. gov/homeandrecreationalsafety/falls/adultfalls.html.

52. "About". 2019. *Possible Pat.* Accessed October 12 2019. https://www.possi-blepat.com/about/.

53. "The World's Smallest Muscleman (Extraordinary People Documentary) | Real Stories". 2019. *Youtube.* Accessed October 12 2019. https://www. youtube.com/watch?v=z-6zRlW7QHI.

54. Reference, Genetics. 2019. "MOPDII". *Genetics Home Reference.* Accessed October 12 2019. https://ghr.nlm.nih.gov/condition/ microcephalic-osteodysplastic-primordial-dwarfism-type-ii.

A HEALTHY HEART

55. Tipton, Charles M. 2014. "The History Of "Exercise Is Medicine" In Ancient Civilizations". *Advances In Physiology Education* 38 (2): 109-117. American Physiological Society. doi:10.1152/advan.00136.2013.

56. "Biographical memoir of Lawrence Henderson" 2019. *Nasonline.Org.* Accessed October 12 2019. http://www.nasonline.org/publications/ biographical-memoirs/memoir-pdfs/henderson-lawrence.pdf.

57. Mehta, Akul. 2014. "Applications And Example Problems Using Henderson–Hasselbalch Equation | Analytical Chemistry | Pharmaxchange. Info". *Pharmaxchange.Info.* Accessed October 12 2019. https://pharmaxchange.info/2014/07/applications-and-example-problems-using-henderson%E2%80%93hasselbalch-equation/.

58. "History Of Exercise Physiology: Harvard Fatigue Laboratory Influential In Promoting Exercise Physiology Research". 2019. *Human-Kinetics.* Accessed October 12 2019. http://www.humankinetics.com/excerpts/ excerpts/harvard-fatigue-laboratory-influential-in-promoting-exercise-physiology-research.

59. JW, Berryman. 2019. "Thomas K. Cureton, Jr.: Pioneer Researcher, Proselytizer, And Proponent For Physical Fitness. - Pubmed - NCBI ". *Ncbi. Nlm.Nih.Gov.* Accessed October 12 2019. https://www.ncbi.nlm.nih.gov/ pubmed/8735989.

60. "Thomas K. Cureton Jr.; Physical Fitness Expert, 91". 2019. *Nytimes.Com.* Accessed October 12 2019. https://www.nytimes.com/1992/12/24/obituaries/ thomas-k-cureton-jr-physical-fitness-expert-91.html.

61. "Cooper Aerobics". 2019. *Cooperaerobics.Com.* Accessed October 12 2019. https://www.cooperaerobics.com/About/Our-leaders/Kenneth-H-Cooper,-MD,-MPH.aspx.

62. " What Are White Blood Cells? - Health Encyclopedia - University Of Rochester Medical Center ". 2019. *Urmc.Rochester.Edu.* Accessed October 12 2019. https://www.urmc.rochester.edu/encyclopedia/content. aspx?ContentID=35&ContentTypeID=160.

63. "High White Blood Cell Count Causes". 2019. *Mayo Clinic.* Accessed October 12 2019. https://www.mayoclinic.org/symptoms/ high-white-blood-cell-count/basics/causes/sym-20050611.

64. Johannsen, Neil M., Damon L. Swift, William D. Johnson, Vishwa D. Dixit, Conrad P. Earnest, Steven N. Blair, and Timothy S. Church. 2012. "Effect Of Different Doses Of Aerobic Exercise On Total White Blood Cell (WBC) And WBC Subfraction Number In Postmenopausal Women: Results From DREW". *Plos ONE* 7 (2): e31319. Public Library of Science (PLoS). doi:10.1371/journal.pone.0031319.

65. "Physical Inactivity And Cardiovascular Disease". 2019. *Health.Ny.Gov.* Accessed October 12 2019. https://www.health.ny.gov/diseases/chronic/cvd.htm.

66. "12 Leading Causes Of Death In The United States". 2019. *Health-line.* Accessed October 12 2019. https://www.healthline.com/health/leading-causes-of-death.

JUST BREATH

67. Salmon, Paul, Elizabeth Lush, Megan Jablonski, and Sandra E. Sephton. 2009. "Yoga And Mindfulness: Clinical Aspects Of An Ancient Mind/ Body Practice". *Cognitive And Behavioral Practice* 16 (1): 59-72. Elsevier BV. doi:10.1016/j.cbpra.2008.07.002.

68. White, Laura Santangelo. 2012. "Reducing Stress In School-Age Girls Through Mindful Yoga". *Journal Of Pediatric Health Care* 26 (1): 45-56. Elsevier BV. doi:10.1016/j.pedhc.2011.01.002.

69. "Principles And Practice Of Stress Management, Third Edition". 2019. *Google Books.* Accessed October 12 2019. https://books.google.com/books?hl=en&lr=&id=T-hUvwUNjvUC&oi=fnd&pg=PA449&ots=Rj486H-MN-R&sig=qOAIDwImRRYEUpm49xWImChf5uo#v=onepage&q&f=false.

70. Chlif, Mehdi, David Keochkerian, Dominique Choquet, Agnes Vaidie, and Said Ahmaidi. 2009. "Effects Of Obesity On Breathing Pattern, Ventilatory Neural Drive And Mechanics". *Respiratory Physiology & Neurobiology* 168 (3): 198-202. Elsevier BV. doi:10.1016/j.resp.2009.06.012.

71. "Trouble Breathing". 2019. *Mayo Clinic.* Accessed October 12 2019. https://www.mayoclinic.org/symptoms/shortness-of-breath/basics/definition/sym-20050890.

72. Pittman, Roland. 2011. "The Circulatory System And Oxygen Transport". *Morgan & Claypool Life Sciences.* https://www.ncbi.nlm.nih.gov/books/NBK54112/.

73. "COPD | National Heart, Lung, And Blood Institute (NHLBI)". 2019. *Nhlbi.Nih.Gov*. Accessed October 12 2019. https://www.nhlbi.nih.gov/health-topics/copd.

74. "Emphysema - Symptoms And Causes". 2019. *Mayo Clinic*. Accessed October 12 2019. https://www.mayoclinic.org/diseases-conditions/emphysema/symptoms-causes/syc-20355555.

75. Rochester, Carolyn L., Carl Fairburn, and Rebecca H. Crouch. 2014. "Pulmonary Rehabilitation For Respiratory Disorders Other Than Chronic Obstructive Pulmonary Disease". *Clinics In Chest Medicine* 35 (2): 369-389. Elsevier BV. doi:10.1016/j.ccm.2014.02.016.

76. Spruit, Martijn A., Chris Burtin, Patrick De Boever, Daniël Langer, Ioannis Vogiatzis, Emiel F.M. Wouters, and Frits M.E. Franssen. 2016. "COPD And Exercise: Does It Make A Difference?". *Breathe* 12 (2): e38-e49. European Respiratory Society (ERS). doi:10.1183/20734735.003916.

77. Feary JR, et al. 2019. "Prevalence Of Major Comorbidities In Subjects With COPD And Incidence Of Myocardial Infarction And Stroke: A Comprehensive Analysis Using Data From... - Pubmed - NCBI ". *Ncbi. Nlm.Nih.Gov*. Accessed October 12 2019. https://www.ncbi.nlm.nih.gov/pubmed/20871122.

78. Stamatakis, Emmanuel, Mark Hamer, and David W. Dunstan. 2011. "Screen-Based Entertainment Time, All-Cause Mortality, And Cardiovascular Events". *Journal Of The American College Of Cardiology* 57 (3): 292-299. Elsevier BV. doi:10.1016/j.jacc.2010.05.065.

BRAIN VERSUS COMPUTER

79. " Brain Vs. Computer ". 2019. *Faculty.Washington.Edu*. Accessed October 12 2019. https://faculty.washington.edu/chudler/bvc.html.

80. "New Report Finds Teens Feel Addicted To Their Phones, Causing Tension At Home | Common Sense Media". 2019. *Commonsensemedia.Org*. Accessed October 12 2019. https://www.commonsensemedia.org/about-us/news/press-releases/new-report-finds-teens-feel-addicted-to-their-phones-causing-tension-at.

81. Banducci, Sarah. 2019. "News Bureau | ILLINOIS". *News.Illinois.Edu*. Accessed October 12 2019. https://news.illinois.edu/view/6367/334240.

82. Pantic, Igor. 2014. "Online Social Networking And Mental Health". *Cyberpsychology, Behavior, And Social Networking* 17 (10): 652-657. Mary Ann Liebert Inc. doi:10.1089/cyber.2014.0070.

83. "Online Shopping And E-Commerce". 2016. *Pew Research Center: Internet, Science & Tech.* Accessed October 12 2019. https://www.pewinternet. org/2016/12/19/online-shopping-and-e-commerce/.

84. "Teen Cyberbullying And Social Media Use On The Rise [INFOGRAPHIC] - Rawhide". 2018. *Rawhide.* Accessed October 12 2019. https://www.rawhide.org/blog/infographics/ teen-cyberbullying-and-social-media-use-on-the-rise/.

85. "11 Facts About Cyberbullying". 2019. *Dosomething.Org.* Accessed October 12 2019. https://www.dosomething.org/us/ facts/11-facts-about-cyber-bullying.

86. "Cyberbullying Awareness And Prevention ". 2019. *Eluna Network.* Accessed October 12 2019. https://elunanetwork.org/resources/ cyber-bullying-awareness/.

87. "Physical Activity Guidelines for Americans 2nd Edition". *Health.Gov.* Accessed October 11 2019. https://health.gov/paguidelines/second-edition/ pdf/Physical_Activity_Guidelines_2nd_edition.pdf.

FOCUS IN ON A BETTER MOOD

88. "Robin Williams | American Comedian And Actor". 2019. *Encyclopedia Britannica.* Accessed October 12 2019. https://www.britannica.com/biog-raphy/Robin-Williams#targetText=Robin%20Williams%2C%20in%20 full%20Robin,Good%20Will%20Hunting%20(1997).

89. Williams, Susan Schneider. 2016. "The Terrorist Inside My Husband's Brain". *Neurology* 87 (13): 1308-1311. Ovid Technologies (Wolters Kluwer Health). doi:10.1212/wnl.0000000000003162.

90. "Types Of Dementia". 2019. *Alzheimer's Disease And Dementia.* Accessed October 12 2019. https://www.alz.org/alzheimers-dementia/ what-is-dementia/types-of-dementia.

91. "Faststats". 2019. *Cdc.Gov.* Accessed October 12 2019. https://www.cdc.gov/ nchs/fastats/leading-causes-of-death.htm.

92. Lautenschlager, Nicola T., Kay L. Cox, Leon Flicker, Jonathan K. Foster, Frank M. van Bockxmeer, Jianguo Xiao, Kathryn R. Greenop, and Osvaldo P. Almeida. 2008. "Effect Of Physical Activity On Cognitive Function In Older Adults At Risk For Alzheimer Disease". *JAMA* 300 (9): 1027. American Medical Association (AMA). doi:10.1001/jama.300.9.1027.

93. Paillard, Thierry, Yves Rolland, and Philipe de Souto Barreto. 2015. "Protective Effects Of Physical Exercise In Alzheimer's Disease And Parkinson's Disease: A Narrative Review". *Journal Of Clinical Neurology* 11 (3): 212. Korean Neurological Association (KAMJE). doi:10.3988/jcn.2015.11.3.212.

94. "What Is CTE?". 2015. *Concussion Legacy Foundation.* Accessed October 12 2019. https://concussionfoundation.org/CTE-resources/what-is-CTE.

95. "The Aging Hippocampus: Interactions Between Exercise, Depression, And BDNF - Kirk I. Erickson, Destiny L. Miller, Kathryn A. Roecklein, 2012". 2019. *The Neuroscientist.* https://journals.sagepub.com/doi/full/10.1177/1073858410397054?casa_token=5U-bIITdG6OAAAAAA%3A_9I_LESrpWxRHSpcqI-bPEwajTSZ3RDB09m-HyLKjg8065VoogijhNQ9SKD_mMvR_zpXhMn_LAr8sZw.

96. "The Brain-Changing Benefits Of Exercise | Wendy Suzuki". 2019. *Youtube.* Accessed October 12 2019. https://www.youtube.com/watch?v=BHYoFxzoKZE.

97. "2.11 Exercise: Nature's Medicine For Depression And Stress". 2019. *Youtube.* Accessed October 12 2019. https://www.youtube.com/watch?v=PSfeThgivOc&t=211s.

98. "Physical Activity Guidelines for Americans 2nd Edition". *Health.Gov.* Accessed October 11 2019. https://health.gov/paguidelines/second-edition/pdf/Physical_Activity_Guidelines_2nd_edition.pdf

SWEAT OUT YOUR PROBLEMS

99. "Depression". 2018. *Who.Int.* Accessed October 12 2019. https://www.who.int/news-room/fact-sheets/detail/depression.

100. "Data on behavioral health in the United States" 2019. *Apa.Org.* Accessed October 12 2019. https://www.apa.org/helpcenter/data-behavioral-health.

101. "Depression". 2019. *Google Books*. Accessed October 12 2019. https://
books.google.com/books?hl=en&lr=&id=Ntw8AwAAQBAJ&oi=fnd&p-
g=PR17&dq=depression+causes+&ots=IoaBFD6MGK&sig=36H1g-iB-
V7TBbbDHxyDJ8FfxTWA#v=onepage&q=depression%20
causes&f=false.

102. "Kevin Love Opens Up In Exclusive Interview About Mental Health Issues
In The NBA [FULL] | ESPN". 2019. *Youtube*. Accessed October 12 2019.
https://www.youtube.com/watch?v=sW2LVIp9QcU&t=1848s.

103. "Everyone Is Going Through Something | By Kevin Love". 2019. *The
Players' Tribune*. Accessed October 12 2019. https://www.theplayerstribune.
com/global/articles/kevin-love-everyone-is-going-through-something.

104. "Michael Phelps Opens Up About Struggle With Depression | TODAY".
2019. *Youtube*. Accessed October 12 2019. https://www.youtube.com/
watch?v=iQGEc-JD3_g.

105. Wegner M, et al. 2019. "Effects Of Exercise On Anxiety And Depression
Disorders: Review Of Meta- Analyses And Neurobiological Mechanisms. -
Pubmed - NCBI ". *Ncbi.Nlm.Nih.Gov*. Accessed October 12 2019. https://
www.ncbi.nlm.nih.gov/pubmed/24923346.

106. Timimi, Sami, Joanna Moncrieff, Peter Gøtzche, James Davies, Peter
Kinderman, Richard Byng, Luke Montagu, and John Read. 2018. "Network
Meta-Analysis Of Antidepressants". *The Lancet* 392 (10152): 1011-1012. Else-
vier BV. doi:10.1016/s0140-6736(18)31784-7.

107. Khan, Arif, and Walter A. Brown. 2015. "Antidepressants Versus Placebo
In Major Depression: An Overview". *World Psychiatry* 14 (3): 294-300.
Wiley. doi:10.1002/wps.20241.

108 Moncrieff, Joanna. 2018. "Against The Stream: Antidepressants Are Not
Antidepressants – An Alternative Approach To Drug Action And Implica-
tions For The Use Of Antidepressants". *Bjpsych Bulletin* 42 (1): 42-44. Royal
College of Psychiatrists. doi:10.1192/bjb.2017.11.

109. "The Nervous And Endocrine Systems Review". 2019. *Khan Academy*. Accessed October 12 2019. https://www.khanacademy.org/science/
high-school-biology/hs-human-body-systems/hs-the-nervous-and-en-
docrine-systems/a/hs-the-nervous-and-endocrine-systems-review#tar-
getText=For%20one%2C%20the%20endocrine%20system,electrical%20
signaling%20(neural%20impulses).&targetText=Signal%20transmission%20
in%20the%20endocrine,responses%20tend%20to%20last%20longer.

110. "Physical Activity Guidelines for Americans 2ⁿᵈ Edition". *Health.Gov*. Accessed October 11 2019. https://health.gov/paguidelines/second-edition/pdf/Physical_Activity_Guidelines_2nd_edition.pdf.

111. Wegner M, et al. 2019. "Effects Of Exercise On Anxiety And Depression Disorders: Review Of Meta- Analyses And Neurobiological Mechanisms. - Pubmed - NCBI ". *Ncbi.Nlm.Nih.Gov*. Accessed October 12 2019. https://www.ncbi.nlm.nih.gov/pubmed/24923346.

112. "Chronic Stress Puts Your Health At Risk". 2019. *Mayo Clinic*. Accessed October 12 2019. https://www.mayoclinic.org/healthy-lifestyle/stress-management/in-depth/stress/art-20046037.

113. Harris, Alex H.S., Ruth Cronkite, and Rudolf Moos. 2006. "Physical Activity, Exercise Coping, And Depression In A 10-Year Cohort Study Of Depressed Patients". *Journal Of Affective Disorders* 93 (1-3): 79-85. Elsevier BV. doi:10.1016/j.jad.2006.02.013.

114. Dedovic, Katarina, and Janice Ngiam. 2015. "The Cortisol Awakening Response And Major Depression: Examining The Evidence". *Neuropsychiatric Disease And Treatment*, 1181. Dove Medical Press Ltd. doi:10.2147/ndt.s62289.

115. Erickson, K. I., M. W. Voss, R. S. Prakash, C. Basak, A. Szabo, L. Chaddock, and J. S. Kim et al. 2011. "Exercise Training Increases Size Of Hippocampus And Improves Memory". *Proceedings Of The National Academy Of Sciences* 108 (7): 3017-3022. Proceedings of the National Academy of Sciences. doi:10.1073/pnas.1015950108.

SHIFTING FOCUS FROM FATNESS TO FITNESS

116. "Why Fitness Is More Important Than Weight | Leanne Spencer | Tedxwandsworth". 2019. *Youtube*. Accessed October 12 2019. https://www.youtube.com/watch?v=-SLP1BF7KBQ.

117. "Defining Adult Overweight And Obesity | Overweight & Obesity | CDC". 2019. *Cdc.Gov*. Accessed October 12 2019. https://www.cdc.gov/obesity/adult/defining.html.

118. "Here's The One Thing That Makes A Kid More Likely To Be Bullied In School". 2019. *Takepart*. Accessed October 12 2019. http://www.takepart.com/article/2015/07/07/one-thing-makes-kids-more-likely-be-bullied/.

119. Church, T. S., Y. J. Cheng, C. P. Earnest, C. E. Barlow, L. W. Gibbons, E. L. Priest, and S. N. Blair. 2003. "Exercise Capacity And Body Composition As Predictors Of Mortality Among Men With Diabetes". *Diabetes Care* 27 (1): 83-88. American Diabetes Association. doi:10.2337/diacare.27.1.83.

120. "Bulimia Nervosa". 2017. *National Eating Disorders Association*. Accessed October 12 2019. https://www.nationaleatingdisorders.org/learn/by-eating-disorder/bulimia.

121. "Adults Need More Physical Activity". 2019. *Centers For Disease Control And Prevention*. Accessed October 12 2019. https://www.cdc.gov/physicalactivity/inactivity-among-adults-50plus/index.html.

122. "NPR Choice Page". 2019. *Npr.Org*. Accessed October 12 2019. https://www.npr.org/sections/health-shots/2014/02/19/279460759/sit-more-and-youre-more-likely-to-be-disabled-after-age-60#targetText=Researchers%20at%20Northwestern%20University%20say,how%20much%20exercise%20they%20get.

The Mind's Eye

123. "The modern obesity epidemic, ancestral hunter-gatherers, and the sensory/reward control of food intake."Psycnet. 2019. *Psycnet.Apa.Org*. Accessed October 12 2019. https://psycnet.apa.org/record/2012-33465-001.

124. "Why Some People Find Exercise Harder Than Others | Emily Balcetis". 2019. *Youtube*. Accessed October 12 2019. https://www.youtube.com/watch?v=QeIrdqUoo9s&t=477s.

125. "How To Stop Negative Self-Talk". 2019. *Mayo Clinic*. Accessed October 12 2019. https://www.mayoclinic.org/healthy-lifestyle/stress-management/in-depth/positive-thinking/art-20043950.

A SOCIAL INTRODUCTION

126. "Theory – Selfdeterminationtheory.Org". 2019. *Selfdeterminationtheory.Org*. Accessed October 12 2019. https://selfdeterminationtheory.org/theory/.

127. Srini Pillay, MD. 2016. "Managing Your Emotions Can Save Your Heart - Harvard Health Blog". *Harvard Health Blog*. Accessed October 12 2019. https://www.health.harvard.edu/blog/managing-emotions-can-save-heart-201605099541.

128. "Sports Participation And Drug Use Among Young People In Mauritius". 2019. *International Journal Of Adolescence And Youth*. https://www.tandfonline.com/doi/full/10.1080/02673843.2017.1325756.

AS OLD AS COMPETITION ITSELF

129. "Bible Gateway Passage: Mark 3:25 - New International Version". 2019. *Bible Gateway*. Accessed October 12 2019. https://www.biblegateway.com/passage/?search=Mark+3%3A25&version=NIV.

130. "House Divided" Speech By Abraham Lincoln". 2019. *Abrahamlincolnonline.Org*. Accessed October 12 2019. http://www.abrahamlincolnonline.org/lincoln/speeches/house.htm.

131. Szalavitz, Maia, and Maia Szalavitz. 2019. "How Disasters Bring Out Our Kindness | TIME.Com". *TIME.Com*. Accessed October 12 2019. http://healthland.time.com/2012/10/31/how-disasters-bring-out-our-kindness/.

132. "Super Bowl Myth Exposed: These Are Actually The Most-Watched Sporting Events". 2017. *Pennlive*. Accessed October 12 2019. https://www.pennlive.com/sports/2017/02/super_bowl_myth_exposed_these.html.

133. "The History Of The Olympic Truce". 2017. *International Olympic Committee*. Accessed October 12 2019. https://www.olympic.org/news/the-history-of-the-olympic-truce.

134. "Olympics Open With Koreas Marching Together, Offering Hope For Peace". 2019. *Nytimes.Com*. Accessed October 12 2019. https://www.nytimes.com/2018/02/09/world/asia/olympics-opening-ceremony-north-korea.html.

135. "How Ping-Pong Diplomacy Thawed The Cold War". 2019. *HISTORY*. Accessed October 12 2019. https://www.history.com/news/ping-pong-diplomacy.

136. "Study Shows Rapid Rise In Mass School Shootings In The US". 2019. *Phys.Org*. Accessed October 12 2019. https://phys.org/news/2018-04-rapid-mass-school.html.

137. "Orlando Shooting". 1466. *Nytimes.Com*. Accessed October 12 2019. https://www.nytimes.com/news-event/2016-orlando-shooting.

138. "Lebron Says Shooting 'Puts Things In Perspective'". 2019. *ESPN.Com*. Accessed October 12 2019. https://www.espn.com/espn/story/_/id/16157049/ sports-world-reacts-mass-shooting-orlando.

139. "Response to Pulse shooting shows growth, power of soccer in U.S.". 2019. *Orlandosentinel.Com*. Accessed October 12 2019. https://www.orlandosentinel.com/sports/os-orlando-shooting-mls-alicia-delgallo-0623-20160622-story.html.

140. "How Major League Baseball Responded To 9/11". 2011. *Sbnation.Com*. Accessed October 12 2019. https://www.sbnation.com/2011/9/11/2414430/ mlb-response-9-11.

141. "Sports & Healing: How Boston Teams Helped City Heal After Marathon Tragedy". 2014. *CBS Boston*. Accessed October 12 2019. https://boston. cbslocal.com/2014/04/08/sports-healing-how-boston-teams-helped-city-heal-after-marathon-tragedy/.

FINDING A COMMON GROUND

142. Giles-Corti, B. 2002. "Socioeconomic Status Differences In Recreational Physical Activity Levels And Real And Perceived Access To A Supportive Physical Environment". *Preventive Medicine* 35 (6): 601-611. Elsevier BV. doi:10.1006/pmed.2002.1115.

143. Stalsberg, R., and A. V. Pedersen. 2010. "Effects Of Socioeconomic Status On The Physical Activity In Adolescents: A Systematic Review Of The Evidence". *Scandinavian Journal Of Medicine & Science In Sports* 20 (3): 368-383. Wiley. doi:10.1111/j.1600-0838.2009.01047.x.

144. Bowser J, et al. 2019. "Disparities In Fitness And Physical Activity Among Children. - Pubmed - NCBI ". *Ncbi.Nlm.Nih.Gov*. Accessed October 12 2019. https://www.ncbi.nlm.nih.gov/pubmed/29095586.

145. Douglas Holmes, Monica Holmes. 1983. "Differences Among Black, Hispanic, And White People In Knowledge About Long-Term Care Services". *Health Care Financing Review* 5 (2): 51. https://www.ncbi.nlm.nih.gov/pmc/ articles/PMC4191332/.

146. "Fact Sheet: Health Disparities By Race And Ethnicity". 2010. *Center For American Progress*. Accessed October 12 2019. https://www. americanprogress.org/issues/healthcare/news/2010/12/16/8762/ fact-sheet-health-disparities-by-race-and-ethnicity/.

147. "Adult Obesity Facts | Overweight & Obesity | CDC". 2019. *Cdc.Gov.* Accessed October 12 2019. https://www.cdc.gov/obesity/data/adult.html.

148. Yu, Yan. 2011. "Educational Differences In Obesity In The United States: A Closer Look At The Trends". *Obesity* 20 (4): 904-908. Wiley. doi:10.1038/oby.2011.307.

149. "Adult Obesity Causes & Consequences | Overweight & Obesity | CDC". 2019. *Cdc.Gov.* Accessed October 12 2019. https://www.cdc.gov/obesity/adult/causes.html#targetText=In%202008%20dollars%2C%20these%20costs%20were%20estimated%20to%20be%20%24147%20billion.&targetText=The%20annual%20nationwide%20productive%20costs,132%20per%20obese%20individual)16.

150. "Economic Costs". 2012. *Obesity Prevention Source.* Accessed October 12 2019. https://www.hsph.harvard.edu/obesity-prevention-source/obesity-consequences/economic/.

151. "Rise In Unemployment During Recession Linked To Weight Gain In Children". 2016. *The Hub.* Accessed October 12 2019. https://hub.jhu.edu/2016/06/03/recession-weight-gain-in-children/.

152. "Prevalence of Obesity Among Adults and Youth: United States, 2015–2016" 2019. *Cdc.Gov.* Accessed October 12 2019. https://www.cdc.gov/nchs/data/databriefs/db288.pdf.

153. " RISE To Win". 2019. *Risetowin.Org.* Accessed October 12 2019. https://risetowin.org/.

WE COULD LEARN A THING OR TWO

154. "Quality Public Education + Dialogue = Democracy". 2019. *Huffpost.Com.* Accessed October 12 2019. https://www.huffpost.com/entry/quality-public-education-_b_5527806.

155. Arne Duncan, U.S. Secretary of Education. 2019. " Education: The Most Powerful Weapon For Changing The World | USAID Impact ". *Blog.Usaid.Gov.* Accessed October 12 2019. https://blog.usaid.gov/2013/04/education-the-most-powerful-weapon/#targetText=As%20Nelson%20Mandela%20says%2C%20%E2%80%9CEducation,use%20to%20change%20the%20world.%E2%80%9D.

156. "The Open Doors" 2019. *Lonestar.Edu.* Accessed October 12 2019. http://www.lonestar.edu/departments/foundationlscs/CF-Essay_Winning_essay_Tung_Nguyen.pdf.

157. "Economic Report of the President" 2016. *Govinfo.Gov.* Accessed October 12 2019. https://www.govinfo.gov/content/pkg/ERP-2017/pdf/ERP-2017.pdf.

158. Carlson, Jordan A., Alexandra M. Mignano, Gregory J. Norman, Thomas L. McKenzie, Jacqueline Kerr, Elva M. Arredondo, and Hala Madanat et al. 2014. "Socioeconomic Disparities In Elementary School Practices And Children's Physical Activity During School". *American Journal Of Health Promotion* 28 (3_suppl): S47-S53. SAGE Publications. doi:10.4278/ajhp.130430-quan-206.

159. "Move It, Move It: How Physical Activity At School Helps The Mind (As Well As The Body)". 2018. *The Conversation.* Accessed October 12 2019. https://theconversation.com/move-it-move-it-how-physical-activity-at-school-helps-the-mind-as-well-as-the-body-100175.

160. "Physical Education Key To Improving Health In Low-Income Adolescents". 2009. *Physical Education Key To Improving Health In Low-Income Adolescents | UC San Francisco.* Accessed October 12 2019. https://www.ucsf.edu/news/2009/11/4328/physical-education-key-improving-health-low-income-adolescents.

161. Von Hippel, Paul T., and W. Kyle Bradbury. 2015. "The Effects Of School Physical Education Grants On Obesity, Fitness, And Academic Achievement". *Preventive Medicine* 78: 44-51. Elsevier BV. doi:10.1016/j.ypmed.2015.06.011.

162. "The US Was Once A Leader For Healthcare And Education — Now It Ranks 27Th In The World". 2019. *Business Insider.* Accessed October 12 2019. https://www.businessinsider.com/us-ranks-27th-for-healthcare-and-education-2018-9.

163. " Center On Education Policy". 2019. *Cep-Dc.Org.* Accessed October 12 2019. https://www.cep-dc.org/displayDocument.cfm?DocumentID=312.

164. "Shape of the Nation" 2019. *Shapeamerica.Org.* Accessed October 12 2019. https://www.shapeamerica.org/advocacy/son/2016/upload/Shape-of-the-Nation-2016_web.pdf.

165. Portner, Jessica. 2019. " 46 States Mandate P.E., But Only Four Require In All Grades - Education Week". *Edweek.Org.* Accessed October 12 2019. https://www.edweek.org/ew/articles/1993/11/03/09pe.h13.html#targetText=Entitled%20%22The%20Shape%20of%20the,no%20state%20mandates%20for%20P.E.

ACKNOWLEDGEMENTS

As a kid I always dreamed of writing my own book, but I knew the journey but be a rigorous one. I often doubted myself thinking that it would never be possible alone. Through writing *Medicine that Moves You* I learned that I was actually right as a kid. Publishing a book is impossible, unless you have a dedicated team and support system to help you see it through to the end. Through all of your support I am finally able to say that I accomplished that dream, and for that I am forever grateful.

First and foremost, I would like to thank God for continuing to bless me with such wonderful opportunities. Next I'd like to my family who have always supported me no matter what adventure I wound up pursuing.

Thank you to all my editors, and everyone on the New Degree Press publishing team, especially Brian and Eric, for believing in me and helping bring my dreams into fruition.

Finally, thank you to everyone who: gave me their time for a personal interview, pre-ordered the eBook, paperback, and multiple copies to make publishing possible, helped spread the word about *Medicine that Moves You* to gather amazing momentum, and help me publish a book I am proud of. I am sincerely grateful for all of your help.

Sameh Wahba*

Samuel Wahba

Hanan Wahba*~

Sabiha Iskander*

Sara Wahba*

Gamal Graiss*

Diane Graiss

Rita Said

Rami Riad

Andrew Metri*

Clara Antunes

Antonina DeStefano

Brian Costello

Jake Taub

Hannah Dove

Sharon Parsa

Michael Sidhom

Cyril Barakat and Family

Eric Koester

Brian Bies

Bailee Tracy

Jennifer Psujek

Cynthia Maloy

Margaret Connolly

Frank Connolly

Bishoy Tadros

Nader Hanna

Evelene Fawadros

Hanan Youssef

Mary Sarah Georgy

Michael Aleci~

Julia Gillies

Sylvana Toma and family

Krista Lapresti

Brandon Klee

Dr. Jonathan DeFreese

Sonia Bolos and family

Amani Riad and family

Faten Ibrahim and family

Phoebe Metri and family

Nardeen Mickail and family

Carl Treiber

Nabil Graiss and family

Irien Moawad and family

Christina Boutros   Cindy Sidhom and family*

Kathy Moawad   Robby Ruffolo

George Basaly   Mona Ibrahim and family*

Madiha Sidhom Mesiha*   Pat Smith~

Nick Attalla and family   Dr. Lee Stoner

Key:
*multiple copies/campaign contributions
~featured interviewee

www.ingramcontent.com/pod-product-compliance
Lightning Source LLC
Chambersburg PA
CBHW071521180526
45171CB00002B/336